Distorted Images

Distorted Images

Misunderstandings Between Men and Women

Anne Borrowdale

Westminster/John Knox Press
Louisville, Kentucky

First published in Great Britain
by SPCK

Illustrations by Posy Simmonds are reprinted by permission of the Peters, Fraser and Dunlop Group Ltd.

First American edition

Published by Westminster/John Knox Press
Louisville, Kentucky

PRINTED IN THE UNITED STATES OF AMERICA
9 8 7 6 5 4 3 2 1

Library of Congress Cataloging-in-Publication Data

Borrowdale, Anne.
  Distorted images : misunderstandings between men and women / Anne Borrowdale. — 1st American ed.
      p.   cm.
  Includes bibliographical references and index.
  ISBN 0-664-25242-7

  1. Sexual ethics—Great Britain. 2. Sex role—Great Britain.
3. Sex role—Religious aspects—Christianity. 4. Feminism—Great Britain. I. Title.
HQ31.B7244 1991
305.3—dc20   91-251

Contents

Preface

This book began life as, in some ways, a counterpart to my first, *A Woman's Work*. That looked at the idealization of women, and had the original working title, 'The Love of a Good Woman'. *Distorted Images* was to focus on negative attitudes and behaviour towards women – and in my own mind I entitled it, 'The Lusts of a Bad Man'. When asked what I was writing about, I tended to reply 'sex and violence', and that is true to a large extent. But the point has been to explore where the relationship between the sexes has gone wrong, not to scapegoat men.

The subjects of sexuality and relationships between the sexes have occupied many volumes of theology, sociology and psychology, as well as being central for most of us in our daily lives. It is not possible to take all of this into account, but I hope this book will make a contribution to the whole. In particular, I have tried to show how sociological and feminist perspectives have a major role in sharpening up theological thinking. I have begun at this point, rather than with the Bible, or with a review of Christian tradition, because these are perspectives which have often been lacking in Christian reflection.

In one sense this is a book on sexual ethics, for it is concerned with the rightness or wrongness of human behaviour, and tries to suggest more Christian patterns of living. Yet I have not tackled the two preoccupations at the heart of much Christian writing about sexual ethics: homosexuality, and sex outside marriage. Both are relevant issues, as I note at various points, but my particular interest is the distorted relationships between women and men in the world at large, rather than the ethics of who does what, with whom and when. Indeed, although I have not addressed this question, it is worth asking

Preface

why Christians have been so preoccupied with genital sexual activity, and have failed to engage adequately with the wider questions of gender, power and socialization. Much is to be learned from looking at Christian attitudes towards homosexuality, and I have tried to pick this up. I am aware, however, that mine is a heterosexual viewpoint, and my arguments still need developing by those with different experience from my own. I am also white, middle-class and married, and these factors too influence how I see things, however much I try to see things from a wider perspective.

Some of my work for this book has been done as part of my job as Social Responsibility Officer in the Diocese of Oxford, and my thanks are due to the Oxford Diocesan Board for Social Responsibility for seeing it that way. Thanks are due too to Carol Smith, for giving me access to a lot of the work published in the United States on theology, sexual abuse and violence. I am grateful to Elizabeth Nash, Alyson Peberdy, Jan Payne, Hilary Cashman and Jim Woodward for their comments on the first draft, and to my husband Paul for answering so many questions about men!

ANNE BORROWDALE
July 1990

· *Chapter 1* ·

The wrongs of womankind

Woman should dress in humble garb walking about as Eve, mourning and repentant . . . that she might more fully expiate that which she derives from Eve – the ignominy and odium of human perdition.[1]

When I think of all the wrongs that have been heaped upon womankind, I am ashamed that I am not forever in a condition of chronic wrath, stark mad, skin and bone, my eyes a fountain of tears, my lips overflowing with curses, and my hand against every man and brother! Ah, how I do repent me of the male faces I have washed, the mittens I have knit, the trousers mended, the cut fingers and broken toes I have bound up.[2]

If women suffer from sexual violence, or are discriminated against in the labour market, or are the subject of a thousand negative stereotypes, who is to blame? Are women innocent victims of male oppression who should repent of ever having washed a male face, or deserving victims who should repent of ever having been born female? Feminist analysis over the last two decades has highlighted the extent of the inequalities women suffer, and it calls for some kind of reaction. The committed feminist will be angry, the committed anti-feminist will either deny that women are disadvantaged, or believe it serves them right.

Christians are found in both camps, but the majority of them probably regard 'women's issues' as unimportant for society and irrelevant for the Church. They may accept that women should receive equal pay for equal work, and perhaps that women should be encouraged to put themselves forward a little more in the service of the Church. Many Christians would admit that things are not always perfect between the sexes, but feel that if women accepted a properly 'feminine' role, and there was more Christian love and understanding, all would be well. The idea that women as a class are oppressed and have had their rights systematically denied them is likely to be seen as misguided anti-christian feminist propaganda. The label 'feminist' is still a frightening one for many people. During job interviews I have felt I needed to work hard to reassure people that despite having written a thesis on 'feminist theology' I was 'all right really'. I recall a colleague being genuinely shocked at hearing me described as a feminist, after he'd actually enjoyed talking to me. But that fear of feminism can only hamper the Church as it seeks to engage with society. The feminist analysis is of the utmost theological importance, for it names the evil of 'patriarchy'[3] and shows how deeply it is ingrained into individual hearts and the structures of all societies. Christians cannot simply go gently along, justifying discrimination against women in the life of the Church in the name of St Paul or of 'natural differences', and not seeing how this links in with a society where sexual assault or even death come to women daily simply because they are women.

According to some people, we now live in a post-feminist age. The battle for women's rights has been won. Enter the New Man, stage left. Certainly it is possible to look back over the last twenty years in Britain, and see that advances have been made. There is legislation to enforce equal pay and prevent sex discrimination; there are few occupations not open to women. Priesthood in the Church of England provides one notable exception, although women can now be ordained as deacons and may possibly be allowed to become priests in the next few years. Women have a higher profile in public life, in politics, and in the media. There is much feminist material making a serious contribution to both arts and sciences. Important work has been done on the dynamics of the relationship between the sexes. There is a general awareness of feminist principles, and most girls at least grow up with some idea that they are not always treated equally with boys, and that this is wrong.

Moreover, there is some evidence that men are changing their attitudes, particularly towards fatherhood. I have been struck, both in the north and south of England, at the numbers of men in supermarkets tenderly carrying babies and attending to them while their wives get on with the shopping. It is publicly acceptable behaviour from men in a way that was not true in the 1960s. The late 1980s saw films about men and babies, and advertisements featuring tender fathers. Male writers have also begun to identify both the effect of patriarchy on their own lives, and the way in which they perpetuate it.[4]

However, this positive viewpoint represents only part of the picture. Despite the gains that can be identified, it is clear that patriarchal attitudes are still deeply entrenched in society. Equal pay and sex discrimination legislation have not altered the basic inequalities between women and men in the labour market or in society in general. Although women's ordination to priesthood in the Church of England may come, women in ministry still suffer discrimination, as their experience in other churches has shown. Far from progress towards equal rights being consistent, some legislation has been introduced in Britain which creates fresh discrimination against women. For example, under British immigration law, male British citizens are almost automatically allowed to bring foreign wives into the country, but female British citizens face additional difficulties if they wish to bring foreign husbands here. This is particularly the case for women of colour.[5]

Masculinity is still bound up with competitiveness and aggression, and even the New Man does not seem to have changed his lifestyle to any great extent. Although there is a slight increase in the numbers of people who think household tasks *should* be shared equally, this actually happens in only around 12 per cent of households (and men are more likely to say tasks are shared than are women).[6] Negative attitudes to women are everywhere. It may not be altogether appropriate to speak of a male backlash against feminism, since male hostility to women long predates feminism. But some feminists point to an increase in violence against women and increased denigration of the female body in pornography, as evidence that men fear and hate women to an even greater degree. It is worrying that the idea that feminism has 'won' gets used to oppress women further by withdrawing safeguards they still need. For example, some divorce reformers want to restrict women's access to financial support after divorce, because 'women are equal'. Yet marriage and child care still disadvantage women in the labour market, and women still earn on average around 25 per cent less than men.

If we look not just at our own society, but around the world, we can see ample evidence that feminism has not 'won'. Seager and Olson draw together statistics from around the world which illustrate the point that

> everywhere women are worse off than men: women have less power, less autonomy, more work, less money, and more responsibility. Women everywhere have a smaller share of the pie; if the pie is very small (as in poor countries), women's share is smaller still.

They show how girls receive less formal education than boys, women work longer hours than men, and eat less well. They document the extent of practices like female circumcision.[7] Yet changes are happening as women join together to take action in countries all over the world. The women's movement may have its white middle-class forms, but it is much broader than that.[8]

Many people in this country have little idea of women's particular disadvantage in the world. Christians especially may feel it is unnecessarily devisive to speak about *women's* oppression when men suffer too. But, as Dworkin points out, '"We're all just people" is a stance that prohibits recognition of the systematic cruelties visited on women because of sex oppression.'[9] Women's disadvantage takes different forms, depending on their economic and social status and the culture they live in. But each woman shares the experience of living in a world dominated and defined by men. It is important for Christians to recognize what this means in British culture, as well as to be aware of the more severe suffering faced by women across the world.

It is also important to see how racism combines with sexism to mean that women of colour are doubly oppressed, and that

4

white women are part of the problem. Political ideology and economic forces keep significant numbers of women in poverty, often with children to support. In the face of such urgent issues, it may seem irrelevant to discuss such apparently trivial matters as sexist language or soft porn pin-ups. Further, it may seem naive to call for better relationships between the sexes as if all would be well if only we all loved one another. I would argue that describing the trivial 'microinequities',[10] as I do here, is essential, for it shows how deep-seated and widespread negative attitudes towards women are. These negative attitudes, and the distorted relationships they foster, affect our life at every level. In particular, they have an effect on, and find an expression in, sexual relationships. And it is not only women who are denigrated. Prevailing attitudes to masculinity are appalling: if that is what men are really like, what hope is there of women and men ever living in the communion to which God calls us? Neither accepting that men are naturally nasty, nor blaming them for all evil in the world, takes us nearer this ideal. We need an analysis that insists on men taking some responsibility for the present state of affairs, whilst not representing women as saints.

It is customary to say that women are viewed in terms of two extremes. They are either idealized as saints, or virgins or self-sacrificing mothers – and in the case of the Virgin Mary, all three; or they are denigrated as evil temptresses, immoral and selfish, prostitutes.[11] Yet it is not simply that there are opposite ways of viewing women, for the two are closely connected. The mother is despised at the same time that she is valued, for her limited outlook and her inability to let her children go. The prostitute can also be seen as woman in her service role, putting the man's desires first, being what he wants her to be. We need to be aware of how both negative and idealized views of women come together to prevent women being seen as ordinary people, sharing a common mixed-up humanity with men.

Understanding is the first step towards changing a situation. But effective change can happen only when an alteration in people's attitudes goes alongside action on the political, structural level. Laws are needed to guard rights and liberties, but they will not work if people do not believe in the principles behind them. It is vital that Christians are involved in action at this level, and one thing we can bring to this is a theological analysis of what is happening between the sexes.

In doing this, it must be admitted that Christianity has a great deal to answer for. If I have shocked Christians by turning out to be a feminist, I have also shocked feminists by turning out to be a Christian. How, I have been asked, can I possibly follow such a male-dominated religion which has been so influential in the oppression of women over the centuries? I have been brought up short by Brown and Bohn's suggestion that women who stay in the Church give the same reasons for doing so that battered women give for staying in an abusive relationship: 'they don't mean it; they said they were sorry and would be better; they need me/us, we can fix it if we just try harder and are better; I'd leave but how can I survive outside; we have nowhere else to go.'[12] That is probably too extreme a parallel; for most women, being in the Church is more like being married to an insensitive but well-meaning male chauvinist than to a physically violent man. And yet Church teaching on female submission even to violent husbands, and restrictive attitudes to female sexuality and reproduction, have led to acute suffering for women. And women who stay uneasily in the Church do need to look at the reasons they give.

All too often, mainstream Christianity has upheld the status quo of unequal relationships between women and men, and supported unjust systems of domination: men over women, white over black. Theologians today need to put that right. I hope this book can make a contribution to that process by pointing a way forward in the area of relationships between the sexes. It will, I hope, have wider implications too, for as Ruether points out, 'the struggle against sexism is basically a struggle to humanize the world, to humanize ourselves, to salvage the planet', and to be in a right relation to God.[13]

Chapter 2

Nevertheless a woman

Men may cook or weave or dress dolls or hunt humming birds but if such activities are appropriate occupations of men, then the whole society, men and women alike, notes them as important. When the same activities are performed by women, they are less important.[1]

Although she was a most extraordinary creature similar to Adam as far as the image of God is concerned, she was nevertheless a woman.[2]

'*All* women are oppressed,' said a friend, standing at the church door after preaching at a Women's World Day of Prayer service. 'Surely, not in Stoke Poges?' came the reply. 'Yes, even in Stoke Poges.' In such a respectable village, it seemed hard to believe. Many women do not feel that they are discriminated against. Though their lives have a different pattern from men's, this feels fairly comfortable. Men might be difficult occasionally, but women expect that! The feminist assertion that we live in a culture which despises and devalues women is often denied by women who think it cannot be true if *they* have never had a problem. For other women, this idea immediately rings true with their own experience. Yet whether or not they perceive a problem, there can be few women whose lives are not influenced to some degree by negative male attitudes and behaviour towards them, even in Stoke Poges.

This is seen at its most obvious in the way that women and girls restrict their behaviour through fear of male violence and abuse. They may avoid walking alone after dark, or being alone with a man in a train carriage, for example. It is very rare for women to be attacked by an unknown stranger in this way. Yet the lurking sex-fiend lives at the back of most women's consciousness (as well as behind the dark trees at the end of my garden!), and cramps their lives through fear. The more extreme manifestations of male hostility towards women are looked at in more depth in later chapters. But in order to understand them, it is necessary to look at the general attitudes towards women of the society in which such things take place.

There are many different explanations as to why there is so much devaluing of female experience. Though we cannot isolate single causes, we can identify factors which reinforce this attitude, and reduce their influence. One of these is sexist, or exclusive, language. It is an odd issue, for, as Janet Morley points out, it has at its heart 'the paradoxical insistence that, on the one hand, the issue is too trivial to be discussed and, on the other, that to raise it is positively satanic'.[3]

A common reaction to those who raise questions about exclusive language is that they are causing unnecessary trouble and hindering communication. I attended a course at which a television producer said that he would carry on using terms like 'the man in the street', because no one objected. He added that the only ones who did object were strident feminists. Labelling any objectors thus, meant he could conveniently discount what they were saying. Most course members agreed with him, but later found themselves amending their language. 'The man in the street, or indeed the woman in the street', said one in a filmed presentation – and completely lost his train of thought. 'Man' had suddenly ceased to be generic. To be made aware like this *is* disturbing, for once we start to notice exclusive language it intrudes at every point, and there is no going back.

One of P. G. Wodehouse's characters sums up the problem: 'Pronouns are the devil aren't they? You start saying "he" and "his" and are breezing gaily along, and you suddenly find you've got everything all mixed up.'[4] We get mixed up not only because there are sometimes practical difficulties in removing sexist language, but because questions about language affect us at a very deep level. Even such topics as split infinitives and mispronunciations arouse great passion. So it is not surprising that we feel strongly about language that relates to our sexual identity as women or men. Anthropologists deduce information about a race's culture and beliefs from studying their language; yet many people are reluctant to look at what 'he/man' language is saying about *our* culture. For feminists, 'that our language employs the words *man* and *mankind* as terms for the whole human race demonstrates that male dominance, the IDEA of masculine superiority is perennial, institutional, and rooted at the deepest level of our historical experience.'[5]

Though that may seem over-stated, historically it is true that women belonged to men, and were represented by them. Some Christians argue that the male sex properly represents humanity, because God designed things that way.[6] Other people argue that it is correct grammar to use 'he/man' language generically, and that it has nothing to do with devaluing women. But many studies have shown that people actually think of males when they say 'he', and this usage is gradually decreasing as people become aware of its inadequacy. We may in time get rid of incongruities like the one in my former local library in Norton-on-Tees, which put all its feminists books under the bold heading 'MAN AND SOCIETY'.

The effect of exclusive language is to devalue women by making them invisible or abnormal in a world which is male until proved otherwise. We recognize the effect of naming in other circumstances. When several organizations get together, and one of them wants to use its name as the name of the larger group, the others are up in arms. They suspect that their own identity would be lost, and that the group whose name was used would become much more important. This concern was very evident in the 1980s, in the heated discussions amongst Liberals and Social Democrats over the name for their new merged political party. Whatever explanations are given, it is inevitable that using 'he' or 'man' to refer to women obscures their identity and reinforces the idea that men are more important.

Similarly, children's books almost overwhelmingly feature male characters, whether human, animal or machine. 'Mr

Wiggle Worm', sings my daughter. 'Worms aren't boys, they're hermaphrodites,' I tell her sternly, but she is not impressed. The Bible stories we tell to children are rarely about girls or women. Sexism in children's books may seem like a minor issue, yet it is harmful because it reinforces the stereotype of the female as passive, and any girl or woman who is adventurous as deviant in some way.

Stories and language have a special significance in liberation struggles – as can be seen from the experience of Black slaves in America,[7] and indeed of the people of Israel in the Old Testament. If women are to fight against poverty, violence, or discrimination, they need self-confidence. And that is harder to come by if they grow up hearing that anything active is male, and females merely lie around waiting to be rescued. It can also lead to women who are themselves strong and active despising their own sex as weak.

These are important issues for Christians, for they relate to the horror many people feel at the thought of calling God 'She', or even talking of sisters as well as brothers in Christ. It is acceptable to speak of God with inanimate names such as 'Rock', but not 'Mother', despite the precedents in Bible and tradition. Christ can be depicted on the cross as a Korean worker, or an Indian, but not as a woman. Yet women too have been crucified with Christ, and Christ is crucified in the suffering endured by women just as much as in that of men. However reasoned arguments against recognizing the feminine aspects of God may appear, they have at their root the notion that it devalues God to use feminine imagery.

But what message is given about the value of women when we call them men, and say that it is blasphemy to ascribe any feminine names to God? Is it not more blasphemous to think that God has a fixed gender? The early Church fathers may have railed against women, but they did have a right appreciation of the transcendence of God. They would have been horrified at the literal understanding many have of our masculine names for God: 'I want a male husband, my God is male, they both value me for being that unique being, a woman.'[8]

Language reflects the belief that men represent the norm. That belief is pervasive in our society. It means that women are seldom treated as ordinary human beings who might think and feel and react in similar ways to men; but as peculiar feminine creatures who act according to some strange internal logic that men cannot understand. Women may be presented as 'a kind of monstrous puzzle that God has created for men to wrestle with hopelessly. We can even be proud of *not* understanding them, for the failure to understand women is the ultimate proof of our masculinity.'[9] Men frequently make joking remarks of this sort about women, but more seriously it may underlie formal assessments of women's behaviour.

Oakley's study on motherhood and childbirth is interesting in this context.[10] She points out that women are treated as if their behaviour were peculiarly *feminine*. It is their hormones, or some emotional instability in the female character, which dictates how they feel. But Oakley shows that women are actually reacting in a very *human* way to a situation which, though specifically female, has parallels with other, shared human experiences. A woman who has left her job to have a baby shares similar feelings to that of someone who retires. The mixture of euphoria and depression which can follow a birth parallels that felt by anyone who has gone through a tremendous experience. Women's behaviour in hospital after having a baby can be a reaction to being institutionalized, like that which other hospital patients experience.

Women react in different ways to giving birth, and there are hormonal and physical adjustments to be made. But if women are only seen as behaving in a particular way because 'women are like that', it prevents any attempt to change the situation. Moreover, such an attitude devalues the positive qualities women can show in childbirth. They may pass through hours of intense agony, to hear that women bear pain more easily than men, and the classic, 'It's much worse for the one watching.' It is a common joke, especially amongst women, to speculate on what the world would be like if men were the ones who went through pregnancy, childbirth or menstruation. The usual point is that these experiences would then be seen as incredibly difficult and vitally significant. Men who had the worst ordeals would be heroes, and labour would be an Olympic sport, though definitely not drug-assisted.

It is as Mead noted. The activities performed by men are deemed significant, those performed by women are much less important. Posy Simmonds makes a similar point about the status of girls in 'Aaah . . . but she's gorgeous!' Numerous studies have found that, where people are given an identical piece of work to judge, those who think it is by a woman rate it lower than those who think it is by a man. Studies in education have shown that even where girls seem to be ahead, they are not given the full credit. One primary school teacher, when asked who got the best results replied, 'Definitely the girls, but I think it's more to do with wanting to please rather than being intelligent.'[11] Girls are likely to underestimate themselves, and to see any success as due to luck. Boys are likely to overestimate themselves, and to see any failures as merely unlucky.

It is worrying to see how little many women value themselves. Not only do they underestimate their intelligence, but in a culture which celebrates health and fitness, millions of women are not happy about their bodies. The images of women fed to us through advertising provide a standard against which women judge themselves, and are judged. Many women have eating disorders, their relationship with food is fraught. Some live continually going on diets, over-eating, then back on the diet, even though this kind of dieting makes any problems worse. A lot of them are not noticeably overweight, yet so many women find it hard to accept themselves as they are. Women may feel guilty at enjoying food, though they are encouraged to spend time preparing it lovingly for their families. Christian women are not markedly different. When they gather together to eat, cries of 'I shouldn't' fill the air just as much as at any secular event.[12] Jesus' words in Matthew 6.25 about having no anxiety about what to eat were addressed to those who might worry about going short, yet need taking to heart by affluent people too. Over-indulgence is never right, but gratitude for, and enjoyment of, what is legitimately ours is part of what we are made for.

Women need to examine whether they have a proper appreciation of God's provision for them. Perhaps the baskets full of loaves and fishes taken up after the feeding of the five thousand came from all the women who turned and said, 'Not for me, Lord, I'm slimming'!

Women not only diet to achieve that perfect shape, some spend a fortune on cosmetic surgery, or on creams to keep them looking young. Women are forever dissatisfied with some aspect of their appearance – bottom too fat, breasts too small, legs too hairy. They measure themselves against some image of what women *should* look like, forgetting that there are several different body types, and infinite variations on the human form. Instead of trying to change the images of women that are acceptable, many women spend their lives trying to change their own bodies to fit the accepted norm. Again, Christian women are often caught up in this. At one time they were not expected to take an interest in their appearance – in my distant past I underlined Bible verses about dressing in modest, sensible and seemly apparel and being adorned only by good works (1 Tim. 2.9 – 10), but it didn't last. Popular advice to Christian women today is more likely to say that God wants them to look good, for him and for their husbands.

In a world where millions starve, Western women's preoccupation with keeping young, slim and beautiful seems scandalous; yet given the culture in which we live, it is very hard to be free of it. Women may be too poor to spend anything on clothes, or choose not to take trouble about their appearance, but they are still judged by what they look like. There are some striking similarities between writing about women and current trends in spirituality. I happened to be reading Anne Dickson's book on assertiveness for women, *A Woman in Your Own Right* at the same time as Francis Dewar's *Live for a Change*.[13] Both spoke about spending time in quiet meditation, getting in touch with, and being centred on, your body. For Dickson, this was to discover what you truly wanted. For Dewar, that process was also coming into the presence of God and discovering God's direction for your life. This suggests that it may be particularly important for Christian women to learn to value their bodies as places in which God is met. This is the same image used by St Paul in 1 Corinthians 6.19, of our bodies as temples of the Holy Spirit. But the fact that he used it in the context of sexual chastity has slanted its meaning. The emphasis has been on keeping this temple pure and unused (or virgin), rather than on living fully in God's presence within it.

Negative Christian attitudes to the body have affected both women and men, but women have been seen as representing the evils of sexuality and 'the flesh'. Despite the fact that we are supposed to live in a sexually permissive climate, women's sexuality is still problematic for many. This is explored further in Chapter 6, but aspects of it can be noted here. For current attitudes toward such things as menstruation, menopause, pregnancy or breastfeeding show how far women are from being accepted as equal citizens. For example, menstruation is a perfectly normal female function, yet it was not until the late 1980s that sanitary products could be advertised on television, and even then the subject had to be treated coyly. Girls and women are encouraged to hide their periods; the ultimate horror is to find that blood has come through on to clothes.

Menstruation is generally described entirely in terms of the negative effects it has: depression, pain, increased likelihood of accidents, and so on. Penelope Shuttle and Peter Redgrove give a frightening list of these in *Wise Wound: Menstruation and Everywoman*, but also point out that researchers don't ask for positive effects. Women may feel sexier, or more creative, or experience the menstrual cycle as a satisfying bodily rhythm. A culture in which women's experiences are valued treats menstruation differently, as a significant rite of passage.[14]

Christians still have unhealthy attitudes to women's bodily functions. One argument against women administering the chalice, let alone being priests, is that they might be menstruating or pregnant. One could reply that the God who took human flesh within a woman's womb is hardly going to be shocked at that. Frances Croake Frank makes a powerful point here:

> Did the woman say,
> When she held him for the first time in the
> dark dank of a stable,
> After the pain and the bleeding and the crying,
> 'This is my body; this is my blood?'
>
> Did the woman say,
> When she held him for the last time in the dark
> rain on a hilltop,
> After the pain and the bleeding and the dying,
> 'This is my body; this is my blood?'
>
> Well that she said it to him then,
> For dry old men,
> Brocaded robes belying barrenness,
> Ordain that she not say it for him now.[15]

Actually, many of those who do not believe that a woman can represent Christ have sanitized views of the Virgin Mary, suggesting that she avoided pain and bleeding when giving birth – though presumably she did have periods. In fairness, Christianity has been less prejudiced against menstruation than other major religions, though Eastern, Russian and Ethiopian Churches still ban menstruating women from receiving the Eucharist.

Breastfeeding is another female function still thought of as 'not quite nice' in public. It has often been pointed out that naked breasts are all right in newspapers or art, but not if they are feeding a baby. As with other female bodily processes, the link with sexuality means that breastfeeding is regarded as dirty, or at the least as a very private affair. The thought of a woman breastfeeding in church, even very discreetly, is sacrilegious to some, although religious art has often depicted Jesus at his mother's breast. I remember attending the induction of a new vicar in the north-east who had small children. His wife was sitting in the front with the baby, right under the pulpit from which the bishop was preaching. The baby began to howl. The new vicar's wife did not feel she ought to walk out on the bishop, and in the end someone else offered to take the baby out. She said afterwards that she knew the baby was simply hungry, but she didn't feel she could breastfeed in front of the bishop. Perhaps this is a situation which clergy wives or female ministers should role-play in theological college!

I have heard many Christians claim that, whatever happens in the world outside, the Church respects women, some even claiming that the Church is in the forefront of the women's liberation movement. This is news to Christian feminists, who are more likely to experience the Church as more profoundly oppressive than any other organizations they belong to. The history of the Christian Church as regards women is a shameful one. Women have been attacked as the embodiment of evil, denigrated as inferior beings, and even physically tortured and killed in the name of Christ in the witch-hunts of the fifteenth to seventeenth centuries. Such blatant hostility to women has declined, yet some of what is said against women's ordination in the Church of England seems to express it. I remember sitting through a sermon outlining a vicar's reasons for opposing women priests and feeling as if I had been physically struck, for what he said suggested that he disliked women, and saw no place for them in the presence of God. Several other women felt equally upset, even those who agreed with his viewpoint on women priests.

Even leaving this on one side, Christian churches give a strong message that women are unimportant. Though the Methodist Church in particular has led the way in beginning to eliminate exclusive language, most liturgy in British churches is about men and brothers. Visitors from the United States have commented on how strange this now appears to them. Male clergy can often be heard bemoaning the fact that their congregations are 'full of old women', and women's groups are dismissed as trivial. But these women are the backbone of the Church, and often have great strengths if they are given the opportunity to use them. Older women might receive more encouragement to act, perhaps to follow the example of

Sarah who, according to Genesis 12–17, at sixty-six set out with her husband for the land of Canaan (and at ninety produced her first child)![16]

Many churches place restrictions on how much girls and women are allowed to do within the organization. Sociologists Hearn and Parkin refer to 'the combined power of image and language in dominating and defining women as "pure" and "submissive" in Christian churches' – in physical fabric and sculpted figures, or hymn and service books, or the conduct of services, especially where there are virtually all-male processionals and other liturgical practices.[17]

None of this is to argue that Christians deliberately devalue women, but it is wrong that our faith challenges us so little about our acceptance of current attitudes. It is often said that the Church is in danger of swallowing ideologies like feminism quite uncritically. But for most of its members, it is *anti*-feminism which has been swallowed uncritically. Yet how can we be credible in our Christian witness to the world, particularly in our talk of justice, whilst we continue to deny the full humanity of half our members? The predominant message that comes across in our churches is not that of women and men together following Christ on the journey of faith. Rather it is of a hidebound institution that has to be excluded from the Sex-discrimination Act because it makes discrimination a matter of principle. It can even be said that the Church upholds negative attitudes towards women by giving them religious justification. The next chapter looks at some of the psychological reasons for the denigration of women, and at how Christian thinking has related to these.

Chapter 3

The trouble with women

Romans, if every married man had made sure that his own wife looked up to him and respected his marital authority, we should not have this trouble with women in general . . . We have failed to control each woman individually, and we find ourselves quailing before a body of them . . . Woman is a violent and uncontrolled animal and it is useless to let go the reins and then expect her not to kick over the traces . . . Women want . . . total license. If you allow them to achieve complete equality with men, do you think they will be easier to live with? Not at all. Once they have achieved equality they will be your masters.[1]

Man is willing to accept woman as an equal, as man in skirts, as an angel, a devil, a baby-face, a machine, an instrument, a bosom, a womb, a pair of legs, a servant, an encyclopedia, an ideal or an obscenity; the one thing he won't accept her as is a human being, a real human being of the feminine sex.[2]

An elderly man in a discussion group once pointed out to me in all seriousness that he was not guilty of oppressing women, because he had a female tutor for his evening class, and always handed in his homework promptly. It is very common for men to argue that they do not devalue women because they have good relationships with some individual women. Those women may not always have quite the same view, but it is nevertheless true that many men can live amicably with wives, mothers or sisters whilst having a low view of women in general. Women may feel the same way about men, of course, and that will be explored in later chapters.

The fact that men and women live together in intimate relationships gives sexism a different character from other kinds of oppression such as racism. Most of us spend at least part of our lives living in a loving relationship with someone of the other sex – whether as children or adults. We ought, therefore, to have some knowledge of each other, so that we see each other as human beings rather than as stereotyped caricatures of femininity or masculinity. Yet one of the basic problems between men and women is that they do not understand each other. Of particular concern, because their perceptions take precedence in society, is men's view of women as abnormal, not quite human. I shall argue in the next chapter that women also devalue men as something less than mature human beings, but women's view is not publicly accepted in the same way.

Though it is possible to describe a set of negative attitudes which men show towards women, they are less distinct in practice than in theory. Inevitably they are generalizations. Individual people may hold them unconsciously, if at all, or they may co-exist with other contradictory views. Nonetheless, it is useful to look at such attitudes in a generalized way, because their influence is profound. The principal feature of this male view of women is that men regard women as 'Other', creatures who are quite different from themselves. Christians may point out that this view is evident in the story of the Fall where, instead of admitting their solidarity in sin, Adam points the finger of blame at Eve.

Confirmation of the essential 'Otherness' of woman is often sought through the study of sex differences. Clearly there are differences between the sexes, but, of themselves, these differences do not require that we see each other as separate species.[3] The fact that women and men are not identical makes human existence a lot more interesting, but our differences are not the only things which matter. Great problems are created when the emphasis is placed so entirely on differences rather than on what the sexes share. So, says Michael Korda, when

> most men look at a woman they do not see before them an equal human being. They see an enigma, a challenge, a mystery; the person is obscured by the sum total of their feelings and experiences about women, by a hundred thousand years of legend, myth, comedy and domestic uneasiness.[4]

20

Relationships between the sexes are spoiled when women are seen as 'Other', regardless of whether women are idealized or denigrated. The problem is that they are not allowed to be ordinary and fallible. At its most extreme, the penalty for failing to live up to the ideal is severe indeed. A husband who killed the wife he claimed he loved, after she had an affair, reasoned: 'If you can't put your wife on a pedestal, who can you put on a pedestal?'[5]

There seems to be a fear of women amongst men, which means that whatever an individual woman is like, and however hard she tries to be pleasing to men, she still represents a threat. It may be that it is not only that men like women to reflect them at twice their natural size,[6] but that men see women as twice their natural size – either exceptionally virtuous, or incredibly powerful. Korda reinforces this idea:

> There has always been, in men, an instinctive fear . . . that women are in fact a more successful artifact of nature than men. The complexity of their biology, their miraculous ability to give birth to another human being, the early imprint of a mother's power on every man, all conspire to produce in men a slight feeling of awe about the potentials of women once they are unleashed.[7]

This was Cato's problem, quoted at the beginning of this chapter. Once women are left free to express themselves, they are thought to become insatiable for power.

Ruether makes a similar point in a religious context, where, she says, stories of Eve, Lilith or Pandora see the female as the enemy of harmony. There is thus 'a tremendous male fear of woman's suppressed power, which, having been once unleashed, overthrew original paradisal conditions and introduced disease, mortality, hard work, and frustrating struggle for survival in place of what was ease and happiness in the midst of spontaneous plenty.'[8] Qualities such as irrationality and spontaneity are put on to women, for these attributes threaten men's ability to feel in control of themselves or the world. Thus one man observes that 'A woman can appear to be illogical and utterly irrational at times, at least to the male mind which wants things tidy and logical.'[9] He does

21

not see that the illogicality and irrationality of this statement disproves his point! Men's fears of women and stereotyping of them are *not* reasonable and logical. Posy Simmonds captures this in 'Cheers!'.

The idea that male fear of women is related to the experiences of early infancy is a common one in feminist thought. Rich believes that 'the male mind has always been haunted by the force of the idea of *dependence on a woman for life itself*, the son's constant effort to assimilate, compensate for, or deny the fact that he is "of woman born".'[10] Dinnerstein develops this theme in detail. For her, the 'crucial psychological fact is that all of us, female as well as male, fear the will of woman.' We have a terror of sinking wholly back into the helplessness of infancy. Dinnerstein's analysis makes sense, though we should be wary of reducing patriarchy to a single factor as she does. She believes that shared parenting would end the exploitation of women. For if unjust blame and spite 'were directed simply at parents, not just at female parents (and subsequently their gender as a whole), it could be more consciously identified for what it is – a childish, out-growable feeling – and endured, forgiven.'[11]

It is indeed important that men play their part in child care, for their own benefit as much as for that of their wives, daughters and sons. The fact that men were once mothered by women can lead to damaging dynamics in adult relationships, as I pointed out in *A Woman's Work*. But whilst men's involvement in parenting could well influence attitudes, patriarchy will not be ended simply because early parental figures are male as well as female.

One reason for male fear and denigration of women may be that men are conscious of their dependence on women. For example, men complain about marriage, but benefit from it considerably. According to Bernard, the idea that spinsters are neurotic, and bachelors carefree, is not borne out by evidence. It is as if we need to believe that women need marriage whilst men do not. She therefore suspects that 'the verbal assaults on marriage indulged in by men are a kind of compensatory reaction to their dependence on it.'[12] The way

23

men refer to their wives often suggests affectionate tolerance for a stubborn, foolish and idiosyncratic creature, who can be sworn at, but would be defended against any outside threat. The parallel with the way men speak of machines or dogs is not coincidental.[13] Ships or cars are personified as 'she' particularly when they are erratic and require special understanding and mastering by the male.

The fact that men depend on women as well as oppressing them is important. But this is not to say that all male denigration of women is compensatory; it is too extreme, and too deeply rooted to be seen in this way alone. It is also structural, for patriarchal society benefits from women accepting responsibility for work which men do not want to do, both paid and unpaid. Male hostility towards women may stem from a desire to protect their own interests, particularly where they feel that women are threatening their power. This is a key element in male harassment of women in the workplace and the public sphere.

In the early 1970s, Germaine Greer wrote that women 'have very little idea of how much men hate them',[14] and feminists have documented what seems to be evidence of that hatred through history and in the present day. Male hostility to women comes out most clearly in feminist studies of pornography and rape. Rather than standing out against such attitudes, the Christian tradition offers some of the worst examples of misogyny.

It is often argued that Christianity in its earliest form had a healthy view of women and sexuality. Mind, body and spirit were seen as a unity, and the religious life was to be lived out within just social systems. Then Christianity became entangled with Greek thought and a dualistic understanding of the world in which body and spirit were opposing principles. Man came to be associated with the higher rational, spiritual realm, and woman with the lower earthy, material realm.

Certainly it is possible to trace this development, although it is unwise to assume that we can isolate a 'pure' form of Christianity which we can get back to. The gospel was lived out in a specific time and culture, in which women were regarded as second-class citizens. Jewish thinking may have been relatively enlightened, and avoided a dualistic understanding of human nature, but women were not regarded as equal. Jesus himself clearly does not despise women, but women do not have the primary place in his ministry that men do, and it is difficult to see how they could have done at that time.[15]

Nonetheless, even if we do not see everything after the New Testament as a fall from purity – for there is also much good theology from the Church fathers – we do need to look at the ideas which were introduced. Of particular importance to the way women were perceived was the fear of mortality and corruptibility, from which men sought to escape, as Ruether explains:

> All that sustains physical life – sex, eating, reproduction, even sleep – comes to be seen as sustaining the realm of 'death' . . . Women, as representatives of sexual reproduction and motherhood, are the bearers of death, from which male spirits must flee to 'light' and 'life'.

Women can share in this flight only as 'honorary males', who renounce their motherhood and sexual nature. But women could never quite escape, for their bodies, even if they were nuns, were seen primarily as sexually dangerous to men.[16]

Strachan and Strachan argue that the hatred the Church fathers show is not so much directed at women for being *female*, but because they symbolize the flesh.[17] For the Strachans, this does not excuse them, but it can explain why some of the fathers could have good relationships with actual women, whilst raging against what Woman symbolized. However, if one human is able to treat another in this abstract and destructive way it indicates an inequality of power between them. Women's symbolizing the flesh cannot be separated from men's devaluing of women in general.

The problem lies in our tendency to think dualistically and see everything in terms of opposites. Masculinity and femininity are seen as opposing principles, paralleled by other opposing principles such as public and private, good and evil, superior and inferior.[18] Relationships between the sexes are inevitably damaged by this world view. Dualistic thinking helps us, because it presents the world in very simple terms. Things are either right or wrong, good or evil. This simplistic approach helps us to feel in control in a world of infinite challenge and complexity.

Christians are very prone to fall into this trap. We feel that faith should give us certainty, when the whole point about faith is that it is *faith*, that is, our hope is in something that cannot be proven. Many of us like to be given an ordered view of the world, which tells us what to believe and how to behave as Christians. We feel threatened by the thought that there is not always a clear right and wrong. I remember that when I was studying for RE 'A' Level, I began to draw up a list of the theologians I had to read, which classified them as 'sound' or 'unsound'. I have a vivid memory of sitting on the school bus wondering what to do about Karl Barth! I quickly discovered that theologians could be intelligent on some questions, whilst being inaccurate on others, and gave up the list. But there is a constant pressure within the Church to make rigid pronouncements, which ignore the way that good and evil (and most other so-called opposites) grow together till the end of time.

Many see masculinity and femininity as opposing principles which are of equal value. Jung's description of the masculine 'animus' and feminine 'anima' falls into this category, and the same view is also present in the Strachans' work. Women are said to need to discover their masculine side, and men to experience their feminine side. Roy McCloughry, for example, in a generally useful article on Christian men and masculinity, writes, 'When a man looks at a woman he does not see someone strange to himself but can understand her because she resonates with the female in him (and the male in her with the male in him).'[19] But most of the time we understand each other because of the vast range of human experience and emotions we share, rather than because anything we recognize in the other sex must therefore be 'resonating' with a masculine or feminine aspect in ourselves.

I do not believe it is helpful to put gendered labels on aspects of human personality which are found in both sexes, and which merge into one another, though it is an improvement on making such principles into a hierarchy in which the masculine is superior to the feminine. The attempt to preserve a hierarchy in which men are at the top leads to a misuse of power. Power becomes an instrument of control, rather than a means of enabling others. Under this model, men are constantly afraid that their power is threatened, and suspect women of wanting to over-power them and take control.

Dualistic thinking often goes alongside an image of God as supremely powerful and controlling. He has strict views about everything, and punishes those who step out of line. This is the God who strikes cathedrals with lightning when heretical bishops have spoken in them, or who sends HIV/AIDS to punish male homosexuals. This angry God demands a sacrifice in payment for sin, and Jesus' death on the cross in place of human beings placates him. Such a mechanistic and simplistic understanding of God's dealings with the world is far removed from the complex relationship described in the Bible and through Christian tradition. Whilst we cannot throw out notions of God's anger[20] and power, we need to see that God has other faces. Our God is both creator of all that is, and the one who becomes vulnerable in human form. We can understand our sin as being removed through our death and rising in and with Christ in a dynamic relationship, rather than as an external transaction.

We need a God who can hold our confused and contradictory feelings and experiences, rather than seeing all doubt as sin, all compromise as devilish temptation. For men, there is a tendency to project such feelings on to women. Thus Korda can say that a male chauvinist is 'a man who cannot accept the responsibility for the failures in his own life and therefore assigns them to women'. If, for example, men value self-control as a part of being masculine, the more unpredictable feelings associated with sexuality or aggression will cause concern. Women may then be blamed for causing these

27

feelings by sexual provocation or capricious behaviour. Thus it would be failure to accept their own physicality which led men such as the Church fathers to identify women with 'nature' and its evil consequences. On this understanding, male chauvinism can be seen not as a 'result of ruthless strength and selfishness on the part of men, but the sign of inner weakness, fear, frustration'.[21]

Women may not be denounced quite as baldly by Church fathers today, but the attitudes linger on. Women are still primarily defined by their sexuality, and held responsible for men's sexual feelings about them. A vicar once told me that he objected to female servers because they were sexually distracting, and some clergymen object to women priests for the same reason. As a bishop once said, 'Women, unlike men, radiate sex, and their temperament is inappropriate in church . . . Their ordination would introduce distractions and earthiness into worship.'[22] Yet if this really is the case, the problem belongs to the poor male minister, who must face a barrage of sex appeal from his predominantly female congregation every time he steps into the pulpit!

It is common to hear Anglican Church leaders pleading that the women's ordination debate be carried on in Christian love. They emphasize that it is primarily a *theological* debate, not to be confused by questioning people's psychological motives. As one bishop said, 'We should avoid any denigration of other positions by imputing personal motives or psychological considerations. The issue is a theological one and we need to be theologically serious about it.'[23] It is understandable that Church leaders wish to avoid emotion and conflict where possible. Yet it is clear that women's ordination raises acute issues about our sexuality and self-understanding, and these may need to be challenged. Moreover, theology itself must engage with these feelings. Theology is not about abstract theoretical arguments about the Godhead. It is about the one in whom we live and move and have our whole beings. What is said of God will affect who we understand ourselves to be. We have a great deal of vested interest in theological debates, for they may involve us in radical change, if we take them seriously. The view that theology can be purely a rational activity must be challenged.

It is interesting that feminists are so often told, 'You have a good case, why do you have to put it so aggressively/get so worked up?' For it is not possible for this debate to be entirely abstract and theoretical when it involves us all at such a deep level. Indeed, if the case is put simply as a calmly reasoned argument, it is either not heard, or not thought to be very important. Whatever they say, men often do react emotionally to feminist issues. Some of the men's comments noted earlier are scarcely rational and logical, and men's feelings about such issues, however disguised, may well be related to the way they personally have been treated by women.

Whatever more enlightened pronouncements are made by Christian leaders, the taboo against women being too closely associated with holy things is still strong in some branches of the Church. Women may not be allowed to be servers, or to go beyond the altar rail. Some object to women distributing the pre-consecrated wafer at the Eucharist. It is not just that women should not bring any manifestations of their sexuality into church – as with breastfeeding – but that women actually pollute what is 'holy'. For some years I went to an Anglo-Catholic church where women were only just beginning to play any formal part in the liturgy. I occasionally helped administer the chalice. Once I was beside the altar, seven months pregnant. Not liking to stand out, I had knelt down with the servers, but suddenly realized I could not get up again. The obvious thing would have been to have held on to the altar itself for support, but I felt very reluctant. I am still not sure whether it was just that I thought other people would have been horrified at a pregnant woman actually touching the altar, or whether it was something deep inside me that told me I was unholy. I had not felt that way when pregnant before, and performing the same function in a less 'catholic' tradition.

Obviously many women share this negative view of themselves as polluters, creatures unworthy to touch the holy things of God. As with me, this feeling may lurk within us despite our intellectual acceptance of our worth before God. People often remark with surprise that it is women who oppose women's liberation or ordination even more vehemently than men. If men's oppression of women stems from fear of women's 'otherness', a fear of losing control and identity, and anxiety about depending on those they have been taught to despise, why should women feel the same way? One answer may be that if women want to survive and to be happy in a male-dominated society, they must accept the prevailing opinion. Questioning the set of assumptions on which you have built your life is deeply threatening. And colluding with the system has given many women a sense of power, which they do not want to relinquish.

Another answer lies in Dinnerstein's suggestion that women fear the power of a woman just as much as men because of their experience of being mothered by women. Women are conscious of their own power in relation to men, not only as mothers but as partners – and even as sisters. I commented to a woman friend that my two-year-old thought his big sister wonderful, and that she organized him very well. The friend replied with concern that I should be careful that he was not psychologically damaged by having such a strong female influence on him. Women so easily buy into the idea that we are responsible for men, can destroy or save them by our actions. We tread carefully around their egos, try not to provoke their sexual aggression, support them by reflecting them at twice their natural size. But in doing so, we perpetuate the view that men are not ordinary human beings either. There will be no fundamental change in the relationships between the sexes until attitudes towards masculinity are thoroughly revised.

· Chapter 4 ·

'Men, who needs them?'

How can such a tradition as the noble male – going into space, building mathematical systems, discovering the laws of the universe – exist side by side with the lowly tradition of oppressing women – keeping women out of educational institutions, excluding women from power in governments, and generally treating women as second-class, often less than fully human?[1]

No one is wise enough to know why God made female reproductive organs compact and internal so that woman is physically free to move about unencumbered ... Or why God made the male's organs external and exposed, so that he would demand sheltering and protection from the outside in order that he may be kept for reproducing the race.[2]

There is a curious contradiction in the views of men which society accepts. On the one hand, they are rational, logical, intelligent, creative, strong, technically competent, and born leaders. What more natural than that men should predominate as captains of industry, politicians, surgeons, judges, executives, priests? But then on the other hand, men have animal natures. Once they are sexually aroused – which they are at frequent intervals throughout the day and night – they have to do something about it. They are incapable of forming tender relationships. They are naturally promiscuous. They cannot cope with small children, washing machines or women. They simply do not understand women, even those they live with. Yet if men really are like that, they should hardly be in important influential positions. How can men look after women's interests if they cannot understand them? How can they make rational decisions in meetings whilst suffering from uncontrollable lust? How can they be responsible for mending

31

cars when they are confused by the controls of a washing machine?

Such questions can be answered, but the contradiction between these different views of masculine nature needs to be addressed. Men have been able to be highly selective about which view of themselves they wish to promote and in which context. When it comes to who should get the best jobs, the assumption that men have a monopoly on the virtues which matter is very convenient. Of course women should not speak in public, urged the Scot Fairbairn in 1874, for by their nature they lack the necessary qualities, found only in men:

> the equability of temper, the practical shrewdness and discernment, the firm, independent, regulative judgement, which are required to carry the leaders of important interests above first impressions and outward appearances, to resist solicitations, subtle entanglements, and fierce conflicts, to cleave unswervingly to the right.[3]

This attitude is still present in many walks of life, where it is assumed that women do not have what it takes to do a particular task.

But men seem to become different creatures when women are complaining of sexual violence and harassment, or of men's tendency to divorce sex from relationships. What better excuse then, than to say that men are in the grip of biological forces over which they have no control? To some degree, these two views of men represent an idealization and a denigration of their sex, which corresponds to the way that women are both idealized and denigrated, and that theme will continue throughout this book. A major difference is that what I want to call negative qualities in men tend to be regarded positively. Aggression is seen as necessary for success and leadership. The fact that a man's 'sexual tension' can be released instantly frees him from the distractions of emotion, says Plattner: 'He is able to concentrate on factual or spiritual matters, to take an interest in things from which sexual love is wholly excluded . . . he will engage in scientific work, solve intellectual or technical problems, in short, pursue his occupation.' A woman's erotic feeling, on the other hand, is always present, so 'there is nothing purely objective, purely scientific, purely businesslike for her'.[4] This is curious, since it is men who are supposed to think about sex all the time, and it is not usually supposed to debar them from pursuing businesslike or scientific occupations.

Plattner's reasoning illustrates the way that facts and ideas about men get interpreted favourably, whilst what is said about women tends to disadvantage and restrict them. This may explain why large numbers of women are unhappy about the positive and negative female stereotypes, with most men seemingly unperturbed by male stereotypes, at least in public. Men may acknowledge that it is wrong to oppress women, and some may feel limited by stereotyped masculinity, but they still benefit from being male in a society which makes men of such central importance.

The assumption that what men do is much more important than what women do is deeply ingrained in society. It emerges in a variety of ways. For example, women's work in the home is devalued, and counts for nothing when they are applying for jobs. Women's sport gets very little attention on television, even though it can be just as exciting as men's, with as much technical skill. Both academic studies and casual observation show how men dominate mixed-sex conversations, whilst women draw them out and listen attentively. I know I perform this role time and again, frustrated, but unable to stop myself reflecting back men's perceptions. And even men's failings and vices seem to add to their importance. A now discredited research finding, seized on eagerly some years ago, suggested that the highest achievers and the lowest failures were male, whereas women clustered around the middle, and were mediocre.[5] In Christian terms, it is interesting that Eve is not the representative sinner, despite being condemned as more sinful than Adam. Perhaps to give her this 'honour' would be to make her too important!

Men seem to have a great deal invested in proving themselves to be different from women, and superior in every area where it matters, in order to know themselves as masculine. Some societies use elaborate rituals to initiate men and women into their appropriate male or female roles. Menstruation and childbirth serve to mark women as feminine, but defining the male role satisfactorily is problematic. Mead points out that many societies 'have educated their male children on the simple device of teaching them not to be women, but there is an inevitable loss in such an education, for it teaches a man to fear that he will lose what he has, and to be forever . . . haunted by this fear.'[6]

Chodorow argues that, in Western culture at least, children associate their mothers with babyhood, and a lack of independence. For a boy, dependence on his mother, attachment to her, and identification with her represent not being masculine as well. So, says Chodorow,

> A boy represses those qualities he takes to be feminine inside himself, and rejects and devalues women and whatever he considers to be feminine in the social world . . . Boys define and attempt to construct their sense of masculinity largely in negative terms. Given that masculinity is so elusive, it becomes important for masculine identity that certain social activities are defined as masculine and superior, and that women are believed unable to do many of the things defined as socially important.[7]

If Chodorow is right, it is not surprising that women's fight for equality poses a threat to men. If women are equally intelligent and able, do the same jobs, excel in sport, and even take up arms and fight, what is left for men? It may be particularly threatening where women combine these capabilities with marriage and child-rearing, for they demonstrate that masculine activities are compatible with, rather than opposite to, the feminine role.

Boys and men need to be able to establish a masculine identity which is not based on devaluing the feminine. This is difficult, as feminist parents have discovered. Discouraging traditional boyish behaviour may leave a boy isolated amongst his peers. Children may become more anxious about gender roles where sex differences are eliminated. It helps the process if boys have a real, positive male figure to model themselves on, suggests Ingham in her study of men. If such a person is not available, perhaps because their fathers are not close to them, they are likely to emphasize what is not-female, and model themselves on a two-dimensional cultural stereotype of masculinity. 'Because of their hunger and unfulfilled need for an image of maleness,' she believes, 'boys are much more susceptible than girls to the negative effects of sex role conditioning . . . Boys are much more likely to conform to the socially acceptable image of what it means to be a man in order to complete their own sense of gender identity.'[8]

A number of Christians pick up the theme that boys need a good male role model. 'No matter what else any man may or may not have attained in this life, if he's helped turn boys into men, he can know that he's not lived in vain,' writes Annetta Bridges.[9] But we need to ask what being a man means. Unfortunately, the picture of masculinity put forward tends to be stereotyped, or to pick qualities actually appropriate for both sexes. In the same book, David Augsburger suggests that to be a man is

to possess the strength to love another,
Not the need to dominate over others.
. . . to experience the courage to accept another,
Not the compulsion to be an aggressor.
. . . to keep faith with human values in relationships,
Not to value oneself by position or possessions.
. . . to be free to give love
And to be free to accept love in return.[10]

He is quite right about what manhood is *not*, but the qualities he affirms are marks of the mature human being, not simply of the mature man. Clearly men and women are different, and their experiences of the world are different; but it is difficult to establish characteristics that define masculinity or femininity.

Jonathan Inkpen explores this dilemma in his paper on Christ as the 'Tender Comrade', whose mature manhood men should seek to emulate, but who is also a model of mature humanity for both sexes. For him, Christ is both vulnerable and strong, tender and tough, and mixes with women as equals.[11] Yet Jesus offers a good male role model, not because he demonstrates some peculiarly masculine characteristics, but because he is a fully rounded, mature human being – and that is what men should aim to become. This area is a difficult one, because attempts to make points about Jesus' maleness inevitably make women's relationship with him less full. It is only a short step from there to excluding women from priesthood because they are not male.

It is interesting to speculate how far the maleness of Christ and exclusively male language for God bolster up masculine identity. Many women have spoken about how it feels to see God always in masculine terms – some valuing it, others finding it wounds them deeply because of what it says about femaleness. Some men accept that exclusively masculine language for God can hurt women, but there is still comparatively little discussion by men of how male language for God affects *them*. Perhaps most do not think about it, since there is no clash between their male identity and belief in a 'masculine' God. Brian Wren's book *What Language Shall I Borrow?* makes an important contribution here, noting the way that men can see a male saviour as 'one of us'. However uncomfortable it is for many Christians to accept, it surely must affirm men's sense of identity to hear God spoken about in male terms and deliberately *not* in female terms.

With Brian Wren, James Nelson is one of the few male theologians who have tackled this subject. He is highly critical of the way male symbols are used of the Godhead: 'When God became male, males were divinized, and patriarchy had cosmic blessing.' He suggests that men project a particular image on to God. Men, he says, have an internal image of a father as distant, wounded, and angry, and sense that God must be like this: distant, cold, controlling and unavailable. Though of course women too may experience their fathers like this. Nelson argues that 'there are distinctive experiences that boys and men have *precisely because of* their male bodies', and that these experiences have importance for their spirituality. He writes that, 'If the woman senses her sexuality as more internal and mysterious, a man is inclined to experience his sexual body not so much as that which contains mystery within but more as an instrument for penetrating and exploring a mystery essentially external to himself.' This encourages him to perceive God as transcendent, someone 'out there'. Male-oriented theology and spirituality likes to speak of ladders, and hierarchies. Nelson draws on Robert Bly's image of nourishing and spiritually radiant, powerful, dark energy in the male which lies in the deep masculine, rather than in the feminine part of man's nature.[12]

I find myself to be uneasy at this labelling of forms of spirituality as masculine or feminine. And it is questionable whether women really experience their own sexuality as internal and mysterious – that is rather how men see it. Yet it is entirely possible that our experiences of our bodies lead us to reflect in different ways about God. If this is so, other experiences besides being male or female will be influential, for example, age, or disablement. But it is important that we listen to each other's experiences, rather than try to lay down how we *ought* to relate to God. An exercise I have tried with various different groups asks them to draw what they think of when they think of God. This shows very clearly that people's experience ranges very wide, and is influenced by other factors than their sex – including the multi-hued nature of God.

It is highly unlikely that the language used of God in most churches will change to any great extent. But it is important that we cease to regard males as inherently God-like and centrally important. Women need to stop reflecting back a distorted picture of men's importance, as Virginia Woolf said:

> Women have served all these centuries as looking-glasses possessing the magic and delicious power of reflecting the figure of man at twice its natural size . . . it serves to explain how restless they are under her criticism . . . For if she begins to tell the truth, the figure in the looking-glass shrinks.[13]

Feminists are not immune to this. When focusing on male violence, for example, it is easy to fall into the trap of believing that men are all-powerful and women helpless victims.

It would seem obvious that men are not uniquely important in a world composed of two sexes, yet to say so is perceived as radical. Men are ordinary. Their needs do not always have priority, their definitions of the world are not universal but limited, reflecting their own particular position and special interests. What men say is valid, but not necessarily universally true. They are not the perfect pinnacle of God's creation, but ordinary, fallible human beings, like women. James Nelson suggests that fear of failure is a strong motif in men's lives, and is connected with performance anxiety over sexual intercourse: 'The potency/impotency syndrome becomes symbolic of life itself for one conditioned in the masculine mode . . . failure always lurks in the shadows.'[14] This may help to explain why so many men feel the need to hold on to an image of themselves as superior, but it also highlights some of the stresses men are under. They are expected to push for promotion and achievement, yet can rest only when they reach their level of *incompetence*, according to organizational 'law'.

Men may feel that being seen as less important is the same as being seen as of no importance, and accuse women of wanting to dispense with them altogether. I would like to be able to say that this is not true; that most women are anxious for good, equal relationships with men, and criticize male behaviour only in order to pursue this aim. Much of the feminist critique is constructive in this sense. Yet it cannot be denied that elements both in feminist thought and in female culture generally despise and denigrate men. Whether men are seen as malicious and violent, or pathetic and incompetent, a low view is taken of the male sex. Amongst groups of women, it is common to hear variations of the sentiment: 'Men! Who needs them?' Just as men have felt for centuries that on the whole, women were inferior beings so, deep inside, I suspect that most women feel that they are superior to men. Granted, there are some heroic and important tasks that men do well, but even so, it is felt, they need the support of women somewhere along the line. It may be almost as hard for women to regard men as their equals as it is for men to regard women as equals.

In our society, many women still want men to provide economic security and to father their children. This may be disguised by talk of love and marriage, but few men are able to satisfy women's emotional needs properly, and men's practical contribution may be all that is left. Sharpe describes some essays written by girls in 1968, looking into their future. Most predicted having children; but 37 per cent then recorded the death of their husbands, after which they could get on with their lives. Sharpe comments, 'It may be that male fears and insecurities about the protection of their power and indespensability are more well-founded than is generally thought!'[15]

The view that marriage is an economic and biological necessity rather than romantic and affectionate underlies the position of anti-feminist women, as Ehrenreich shows. She writes that such women confine themselves to their traditional roles because they accept 'the most cynical masculine assessment of the heterosexual bond: that men are at best half-hearted participants in marriage and women are lucky to get them.' The crime of feminism is not hating men, but 'trusting them too well'. For inherent in the anti-feminist position is 'a profound contempt for men'. All are presumed to be weak, and 'maintained in working order only by the constant efforts, demands and attentions of their wives'.[16] This view of the sexes is found in many Christian writers too, as I showed in *A Woman's Work*.

Women may privately view men as weak and dependent, but men hold public power, and thus do not need to worry what women think of them. Interestingly there is one area where men are beginning to mind how they are viewed, and that is in the area of violence and abuse against women and children. Perhaps a few men enjoy their power to frighten women. But for most, the suspicion which their quite innocent behaviour can evoke in women and children is a cause for pain. Indeed it should be. What a terrible indictment of men that children have to be taught to fear them; that women will not walk the streets alone because of them; that women are least safe from violence within their own homes, because it is the men they live with who are least to be trusted.

It does hurt for fathers to know that their children need to be warned about what dads can do. Many men say they now feel unsure about how to behave with children, and hold back from contact with them in case they are suspected of abuse. Perhaps in some cases the problem is a real one, but it is also another example of the syndrome: 'It's worse for men', and diverts attention away from the real victims. The question needs raising as to why men do not *know* the difference between abusive and non-abusive behaviour. A child abuse specialist was once asked at a conference by an elderly judge: 'Does this mean I can't share a bath with my little granddaughter?' 'Do you get sexually aroused when you do it?' he was asked. 'Of course not, what do you think I am?' he replied. 'Well then, go ahead.'

That answer is nice and pat, but conceals the complexity of the issue. For there is an element of sexuality in the feelings of parents of both sexes for their children. Women may sexually abuse children with less frequency than men – though perhaps more often than has generally been thought in the past – but women's sexuality is closely tied to bearing children, and they have to cope with the conflicting feelings this causes. Sexual abuse is in any case not simply about sex, as we see in Chapter 10. It is about the misuse of power and the desire to control someone else. It may be that men are particularly vulnerable to this sin, but the reasons are complex.

It may be that traditional masculinity hinders men from forming appropriate loving relationships with women and children, and it is good if some men are able to recognize that patriarchy has failed them too. Korda, for example, writes that men can only justify male chauvinism by saying that it is a social custom too deeply ingrained to be eradicated, and that it *works*. But, he goes on, 'it doesn't. We pay the price for our assumptions in unhappiness, divorce, bitterness, the constant sense of being ourselves prisoners of some system that has separated the species into warring camps.'[17]

It is fairly common now to hear men complain that the masculine role restricts and damages them, so what we really need is *men's* liberation. Feminists are understandably suspicious whenever they hear talk of 'men's liberation', for it tends to be presented as an alternative to women's liberation. In yet another variation of the 'it's worse for men' theme, men's problems become the most important. This proves to be a convenient way of deflecting the discussion from a critique of male use of power, to making men objects of pity. Women are then likely to find themselves rallying round to comfort bruised males, or if they refuse to take this male *angst* seriously, attacked for being heartless. We do indeed need a reassessment of the male role and changes in men's behaviour, but that is a task which must predominantly be done by men. Many men express concern that women will become just like men, with all men's aggression and difficulty with relationships. The answer to that is not that women should accept their present situation, but that men should change. 'Do as I say, not as I do' was never a very good model to offer others.

Unfortunately, few of the men who claim that men need liberating seem prepared to do anything about it. We may see men being more open about their emotions and discovering the joys of fatherhood, but their attitudes and behaviour towards women do not seem to have altered much. Men may be more in touch with their own feelings; they do not seem to be more in touch with women's. It is essential that men actually spend time *listening* to women, and trying to understand what it has meant for women to be subordinate. Without that understanding, the 'New Man' is likely to construct himself a new role that is equally oppressive. Most men do not wish to give up the privileges that go with being male. It is only a few who will actively renounce the patriarchal system; like the male deacon who refuses to be made a priest whilst women are still barred from the priesthood. In Rich's view, 'the majority of "concerned" or "pro-feminist" men secretly hope that "liberation" will give them the right to shed tears while still exercising their old prerogatives.' They are likely to see the women's movement either in terms of men being punished by women for bad behaviour, or as offering the potential healing of men's pain by women.[18]

But both those understandings put all the responsibility upon women, whereas we need men to take an active role in

41

challenging the patriarchal order. Doing that means men accepting some responsibility for the oppressive systems with which they collude. A distinction is sometimes drawn between racism, the way that white structures perpetuate the oppression of people of colour, and racialism, the internal prejudices which many white people have. Both need addressing, but white people cannot be held individually responsible for unjust structures, as they can for their own internal prejudices. Similarly, though individual men cannot be held responsible for patriarchy, they can be challenged about their own sexism. It is important to challenge both patriarchal structures and sexist prejudice, but it is sometimes easier to start with oneself. We all need to examine how we relate to one another as women and men, for our relationships are so often damaged by conscious or unconscious sexism. We are too ready to judge each other on the basis of what gender we are, rather than seeing each other as fellow human beings.

· *Chapter 5* ·

Where women don't belong

If you go around promoting women just because they're the best person for the job, you could create a lot of resentment throughout the service.[1]

This baroque structure of myths constructed over the centuries, is the means by which men cling to their masculine pride while sitting at their desks doing a job that a woman could do just as well or better. But if she could, then who the hell are we? To ask men to allow women into this dream castle is to ask them to dismantle it, to admit that nothing is taking place in this office, at this desk but work without glory, without special significance. Man's world is no longer special, but ordinary, no longer a heavy burden with earned privileges, but merely the same world as every other human being's. As women push into man's world, demolishing the ancient prerogatives, they are destroying man as God, reducing him to human proportions.[2]

Negative attitudes towards women are particularly significant in the sphere of employment. For they can serve to keep women in their own areas, where they tend to be cut off from many better paid careers or more interesting and skilful jobs. Although there are some men or women who do jobs typically done by the other sex, job segregation is very marked. Those women who do traditionally male jobs – in the fire service, or in the building trade, for example – are especially likely to meet with opposition, and direct sexual harassment. Harassment may be particularly severe in the workplace setting because men feel this to be their territory, and resist women's intrusion into it.

The association between masculinity and paid work needs examination if the problems women experience there are to be understood. Men have traditionally proved their masculinity through their jobs. This depends on paid work being perceived as *non-feminine*, since men cannot prove their masculinity by doing tasks of which women are equally capable. The wage packet is the 'particular prize of masculinity in work', says Willis of manual jobs, 'held to be central, not simply because of its size, but because it is won in a masculine mode in confrontation with the "real" world which is too tough for the women.'[3] This can be problematic for men at a time of high unemployment. The association between middle-class masculinity and employment may be less overt, but is equally real. Barbara Rogers skilfully shows the links between the attitudes of working-class men and professional middle- and upper-class men when it comes to excluding women from their particular worlds. The women managers interviewed by Cooper and Davidson felt under pressure from the stereo-typical attitudes of the men with whom they worked.[4]

Paid work can only affirm masculine identity if women cannot do the same jobs, or cannot do them as well. This can create difficulties, since women clearly do many jobs which are highly skilful, or require valuable qualities, or which are sheer hard physical work. Jobs which women do, and the women who do them, tend to be downgraded. Women spending long hours doing boring work in poor conditions are said not to mind. The implication, sometimes stated, is that women are not capable of minding, being unintelligent and naturally suited to such work. Similar attributes are given to minority ethnic groups. White feelings of superiority are confirmed by the belief that Black people cannot do the work. White women may exclude Black women out of a similar desire to preserve the status of a particular job. Women of colour face double discrimination on the grounds of race and sex, and tend to be the most exploited group of workers in Britain.

Masculinity is linked to paid work not only because doing the task confirms masculinity, but because the main male role in our society is to be the breadwinner. Men are still expected to be able to support their families, and if they cannot perform that role, they can feel truly emasculated. This seems to hold for men in all walks of life, although it may be that for some groups beset by chronic and long-term unemployment, masculinity is proved in other ways than through employment. In fact for some groups of women such as those of West Indian origin, it is part of the *female* role to be a good breadwinner. For some husbands, it is crucial that their wives either do not earn, or earn much less than they do. Their masculinity is threatened by their wives' economic independence. This is why some women give up their own jobs when their husbands become unemployed, in an attempt to maintain their husband's ego.

The world of employment as we have it today takes little account of domestic life. Many jobs have developed with the assumption that the worker has a wife at home to care for him, and little desire to spend time with his children. Long or unsocial hours, or the willingness to move or travel away, are written into many jobs. Men have often accepted this as the way things have to be, and not resisted their job taking over their lives. They may even have glorified this as a vocation, as happens in the Church, and left their family feeling that to complain of neglect is to challenge God. It has been clearly shown that there are many interconnections between home and employment for men,[5] but these interconnections are more obvious when women with children enter the workforce. It then becomes clear that children need care when parents are out at work, or that frequently being away from home causes disruption to family life.

It is difficult for either sex to combine employment successfully with family life. At least women have been able to fashion out for themselves ways in which they can spend time with their families, however unsatisfactory these may be: giving up employment completely, part-time working, using child care, home-working, and so on. It is expected that they will do this. But the ideology of masculinity, the demands of capitalism (though other systems are just as bad on this), the work ethic, and material needs, combine to keep men bound to jobs which are damaging in the long term. As Brian Jackson asked:

Why don't men object to this mismatch of public and private life?
. . . Is it simply not knowing what to do about societies which pile
up economic questions in one corner, family questions in another,
obscure one and then establish such byzantine and wasteful
patterns that all either obey or despair?[6]

It is vital that Christians challenge the present situation, and
work for more humane employment practices and better
integration of the public and the private spheres. One might
hope that the Church itself would give a lead on this. Yet
clergy are prone to getting caught up in the 'workaholic' trap.[7]
I remember one vicar telling me how he felt pressured into
working over-long hours because otherwise the men in his
parish would not respect him. Their lives were given over to
their jobs, and whilst he saw the damage this caused them and
their families, he could not challenge it.

The assumption that women do not properly belong in the
labour market has led in the past to a great deal of research on
why they should want jobs, and the effect of mothers'
employment on their children. Because women are needed in
the labour market in the 1990s, these questions have receded
into the background. But the effect of concentrating on them
has been to render women's employment problematic, whilst
men's relation to paid work is left unexamined. Women's
reasons for doing paid work have tended to be denigrated,
though in many respects they parallel those of men. The need
for income becomes in women's case the desire for 'pin money'.
The need to relate to other people becomes the desire for a
good gossip. The need to make a contribution to society
through creative or useful work becomes a desire to get out of
the house. Both sexes gain a sense of identity and worth
through paid work and the social relations they have through
it. Women value the identity and autonomy it offers them,
whilst for men it is associated with masculinity. It is important
to note these shared experiences, for they indicate that the
world of employment is not a male preserve which women
relate to only casually.

Though employment is important for women, because it
has not been central to their sexual identity they are less prone

to letting it take over their lives. Women may use a job as an escape from domestic responsibilities, but are less likely to use it as a substitute for relationships. Warning bells are sometimes sounded about the emergence of a new hard breed of female who abandons her femininity and her family for the sake of her career. There are some women who have bought into this system, and it is difficult even for those who want to do things differently. It still seems to be the case that women need to be better than men to succeed, yet they are blamed for being unfeminine if they do. Nonetheless, a lot of women put a great deal of energy into trying to have both a successful job and a fulfilled family life – and that is why so many women feel under pressure.

Women are often associated with the gentler virtues of caring and tenderness, and this leaves men free to pursue success in a harsh, competitive world. But if women too are seeking only fulfilment, wealth and ambition, society seems doomed. Michael Korda reflects this when he writes: 'The unfamiliar spectacle of a woman ignoring her children to make business trips, focusing her life on success, is an uncomfortable demonstration of just what we, as men, have done in the service of our careers.'[8] The answer is not to discourage women from having careers, so that they may continue to be the carriers of virtue, but to challenge damaging patterns of work and encourage men to change their behaviour. At its most patronizing, men could think in terms of setting women a good example!

Yet men are not necessarily happy about opening up traditionally male jobs to women. They can cope with one or two token women, for this may even add to the job's status: 'We're open to women, but it's far too difficult a job for all but the most exceptional.' Men may begin to get uncomfortable, however, when the percentage of women grows. If significant numbers of women enter 'male' jobs, the status drops, and it becomes less attractive to men. It is interesting to speculate whether women's ordination and leadership in the Church will eventually turn it into a female 'ghetto', with no men coming at all. Since an all-male leadership has not brought men in, it may be that female leadership would bring *more* men in. They would not feel that the only place for men in a church was up-front.

As women enter larger numbers of male jobs, so the remaining male bastions fight hard to retain their exclusivity by overt or subtle means. Though Korda's language at the start of this chapter is intentionally exaggerated, he expresses the threat well. Many reasons are given as to why women should be excluded from a particular male sphere. In their own context, they may seem reasonable, but it is striking how the same arguments are repeated. The first stage is to say that women cannot do the work, being physically or mentally incapable. John Stuart Mill's point is valid here: 'What women by nature cannot do, it is quite superfluous to forbid them from doing. What they can do, but not so well as the men who are their competitors, competition suffices to exclude them from.'[9]

The second stage is to say that women ought not to do it – because it offends in some way their essential femininity, or God, or both. Opponents of women's ordination often fall into this bracket. The third stage is to agree that there are no theoretical problems, but to highlight practical difficulties. The Church of England was in this position in the 1980s over women's ordination. It is an argument commonly cited in employment. For example, firms will say they would like to bring women in, but do not have the toilet facilities.

Finally, the argument will be that women will not fit in. This is unanswerable in some respects. A good working life is based on good relationships between people. Introducing someone unfamiliar with the 'culture' will disturb things – though of course disturbance can have very positive results. Many of the older professions have their roots in exclusively male traditions, and men within them may fight very hard to preserve what is familiar. Ironically, though the talk may be of preserving standards, totally incompetent men can be protected within a profession for years, whilst highly able women are left out. This is immensely frustrating for women who are outside an organization fighting to get in. It is seen clearly in the Roman

Catholic Church and in the Church of England, where male priests can function inadequately for years in parishes or be put in office-based jobs to keep them out of the way, whilst women are denied the chance even to test their vocation.

There may or may not be a conscious desire to exclude women, but as Mead says, when women try to enter previously male jobs, 'the whole pattern of thought, the whole symbolic system within which the novice must work, facilitates every step taken by the expected sex, obstructs every step taken by the unexpected sex.'[10] It is sometimes suggested that general manners between men and women show that women are felt to be visitors: chairs are pulled out for them, doors held open. No wonder women who feel themselves to be equals find these shows of respect from men unnerving. They introduce sex where it should be irrelevant, and indicate that women do not belong.

Sexual harassment conveys a similar message. Wise and Stanley say that a composite workplace definition of sexual harassment suggests it is 'repeated and unreciprocated actions, comments and looks of a sexual nature and which treat the recipient as a sexual object only. It prejudices the recipient's job security or promotion prospects and/or creates a stressful working environment. Generally the recipient is a woman and the harasser is a man, although it isn't unknown for a man to be harassed.' Yet, they point out, speaking of it in this way separates it off from other forms of sexism, and lets people think it can be solved through discrimination legislation, or tribunals.[11]

I shall look at sexual harassment in that more general context of male behaviour towards women in Chapter 9. But it is worth noting that there may be particular reasons why sexism occurs in the workplace. For example, it may represent a misguided attempt to make human contact (as it may outside the workplace too). Hearn and Parkin note high levels of harassment in industries characterized by alienating work conditions, and lack of control of the product and act of production. They wonder whether 'harassment could be interpreted as an attempt to create some human contact as

49

part of or in reaction to this alienation, or just another alienated working act.'[12]

As Hearn and Parker show, sexuality pervades organizations, and not only in the more obvious ways. Some organizations, such as the pornography industry, may have sexual goals. Others use sex in the course of what they do, for example, advertising, or the use of women to facilitate business deals. Military establishments exploit male heterosexuality through the humiliation and hatred of women. Pornography and the use of prostitutes may be encouraged. Segal asserts that 'military training for men is designed to promote a particular type of aggressive "masculinity".' 'Woman' and 'queer' are the most frequent insults hurled at each new recruit, and homosexuality is illegal. The tough image of military manhood helps to attract recruits, and to 'sustain the morale and self-esteem of the men already in uniform'. Women in the forces are a threat, because their presence threatens that masculine image of military life.[13]

Joan Smith, in *Misogynies*, quotes the mostly unprintable thoughts and fantasies of US bomber pilots in a privately circulated pamphlet: 'The women of their pornographic imagination are objects of desire and disgust, syphilitic hags who "suck out your guts".'[14] Yet at the same time, militarism is justified as the protection of women and children – by the authorities, though not necessarily by servicemen. They talk more in terms of defending their mates, and their attitudes to women may act as a cohesive force. Women themselves often talk about soldiers as 'our boys', and send them off to war or welcome them home with patriotic fervour. It is difficult to know how men in the forces can reconcile these contradictory attitudes towards women, though perhaps it is only a more extreme example of the ambivalent feelings most men have towards women.

Many organizations have unofficial initiation ceremonies that are sexual in tone. These are common in men-only organizations, as well as being part of the culture in women's workplaces.[15] Sexuality is ever-present in organizations, say Hearn and Parkin, yet it can be difficult to pin down. It makes itself felt through ambiguities, innuendo, gossip, and joking, but is seldom talked about publicly and freely. The language and imagery of a predominantly male workplace, 'girlie' calendars, adverts, sex-stereotyping of secretaries, the sneering and sexual joking and horseplay, can all serve to make women uncomfortable whilst affirming men's sense of shared masculinity. Posy Simmonds wonders what it would be like to turn this world upside-down for a moment. The rituals of back-slapping, sexist joking, and the constant reminder of heterosexuality, which characterize men's relationships with one another, make it difficult for homosexuals within an organization.

Such behaviour reinforces the idea that women do not belong. If they join in, they are unfeminine; if they opt out or complain, they isolate themselves. Women may create a similar atmosphere which is uncomfortable for men. But the few men in a female workplace are much more likely to be in senior positions, and less likely to suffer harassment.

Sexual harassment of women is a serious problem in the workplace because the harasser is often in a superior position, and if the victim complains, she is in danger of losing her job. The nature of women's jobs also means they are less likely to be free to move around in order to avoid men who harass them. Sexual harassment is widespread, although it is only in recent years that it has been given public recognition. It is common across all kinds of occupations; one would like to think that clergymen were immune, but many women who work for the Church know better. One woman reported how a man who had been making her feel uncomfortable all week at a Church conference came up to her during the Peace, and offered 'a nice sexy hug', and other women have said they have had problems during the Peace with inappropriate touching and kissing from men. And how is all that to be dealt with in the context of a Eucharist? Sexual harassment may be more obvious to women entering traditionally male jobs, because they expected to be treated as equals. Women in more traditional female jobs often just accept it as normal behaviour from the men with whom they work.

It seems that sexuality in the workplace is at once pervasive, and seen to be irrelevant. The hard-working male manager may see himself as wedded to the job, in which his sexuality has no place. Yet success and career are often seen as indicators of men's masculinity and sexuality. Wealthy men have an aura of sexuality even if they are physically unattractive. This is perhaps another example of a common situation in the workplace, whereby men's weaknesses are interpreted as strengths or ignored, whilst supposed female weaknesses are highlighted and used to exclude them. A similar mechanism occurs when the dominant White group defines Black people as different, and denies them opportunity on that basis. Miles comments that there is a 'quite unexamined and taken-for-granted feeling among men that a woman will always behave like a woman no matter what the nature or demands of her job'.[16] There are a number of versions around of a piece which compares attitudes towards women and men:

He's ambitious	She's pushy.
He's having lunch with the boss – he must be doing well.	She's having lunch with the boss – they must be having an affair.
He gets on well with people at work.	She's always gossiping.
He's moving on – he must be a good worker.	She's moving on – women are so unreliable.

and so on.[17]

Women are highly visible when they step out of their traditional roles. This means that professional women in token or lone positions face strains and pressures which dominant members of the organization do not have: increased performance pressure, visibility, being a test case for future women, isolation, lack of female role models, exclusion from male groups, and distortion of women's behaviour by others to fit them into pre-existing sex stereotypes.[18] These factors operate even where women have been welcomed into a male-dominated profession.

As in their personal relationships, so in the workplace, men and women find it difficult to understand and accept each other. The system of patriarchy affects us all, and distorts our dealings with one another. Once again, we are faced with the knowledge that good will is not enough to allow women and men to live in harmony.

Chapter 6

Damaged relationships

It seems possible that now, for the first time in history, women in substantial numbers hate, fear and loathe men as profoundly as men have all along hated, feared, and loathed women.[1]

[Feminism] presumes a radical concept of 'sin'. It claims that a most basic expression of human community, the I-Thou relation as the relationship of men and women, has been distorted throughout all known history into an oppressive relationship that has victimized one-half of the human race and turned the other half into tyrants . . . Feminism continues, in a new form, the basic Christian perception that sin . . . is not simply individual but refers to a fallen state of humanity, historically.[2]

Why is it that men have dominated over women for so long? Though in some societies the sexes are more equal than in others, it is difficult to find conclusive evidence of matriarchal societies, where women have control over men.[3] Some think that the universality of patriarchy proves that it is either biologically determined, or God's will, or both. Others see it as an indicator of how deeply sin affects both society and individual relationships.

Many different theories have been proposed as to why patriarchy arose. No single one is sufficient as an explanation, yet such theories can help us to tackle aspects of the system. Similarly, labelling patriarchy as sin does not explain it, but does help us in our dealings with it. According to traditional Christian theology, the Fall results in the dislocation of human relationships: 'Our sinfulness expresses itself in various kinds of broken, distorted, perverted, or destructive relationships to our fellows and to the natural world.'[4] At the centre of the story of the Fall is a description of how a harmonious male/female relationship deteriorates to one of domination and distrust. Yet this aspect of the story has not been developed at length within past Christian tradition, which instead generally accepted that woman would have been subordinate to man in some way, even in the original, unfallen, creation. The equality of man and woman in Christ could be interpreted in a spiritual way which avoided applying it in actual social situations.

Christians do point to the fact that sin has damaged relationships between people in general and between men and women, but not enough attention is paid to structures. It is certainly not possible to analyse what is wrong between men and women without looking at the patriarchal system as a whole. I have heard Christians argue that it is sin rather than economic, social or political pressures which underlies the breakdown of relationships, which they see as being at the heart of society's problems. Yet unless we see that sin happens through these systems, we can have no hope of tackling our problems. We also need to see how the oppression of women is linked to other forms of oppression, such as racism. It is as pertinent to ask why human beings in general are so ready to feel themselves to be superior, and to seek to dominate over others, as it is to ask why men oppress women.

Feminist theology has been quick to see in the story of the Fall a condemnation of the present unequal relation between the sexes:

> Where once there was mutuality, now there is a hierarchy of division . . . the woman is corrupted in becoming a slave, and the man is corrupted in becoming a master. His supremacy is neither a divine right nor a male prerogative. Her subordination is neither a divine decree nor the female destiny. Both their positions result from shared disobedience.[5]

If we see the breakdown of relationships as *sin*, we cannot take refuge in the idea that God created women and men so differently that they cannot be expected to understand one another. There is a danger of this amongst those who stress the complementarity of the sexes. Moreover, the damage to the male/female relationship goes very deep. This is clearly borne out in the work done by Shere Hite in her report *Women and Love*.

The picture painted in Hite's report is a damning indictment of relationships between the sexes. Women speak of the callous behaviour of men towards them, even in their most intimate relationships. They describe how the men they live with do not listen to them, always expect agreement, and fail to ask about their activities. Hite observes that men with these demeaning attitudes are not treating women they love with even the courtesy they would show a business associate. And women, she says, are quite unprepared for the feeling that the man they love is using them for target practice. It might be argued that home is the place where men unwind, where they do not have to be on their best behaviour. But women are not asking for impeccable behaviour, merely that they should be treated as people and not as furniture. Men also unwind with their male friends, yet do not consistently ignore or sneer at them.

Hite calls it 'emotional terrorism' or 'emotional harassment' by men. Male nagging often takes the form of subtly belittling women, yet it is disruptive for women to react to what are just passing references and it is seen as trouble-making. Or male nagging may be expressed through silent withdrawal, 'sulking, or silent, arrogant, disapproval'. Hite concludes:

> The general tacit social perception that women have less right to their perceptions, their selfhood, than men do, and the oblique ways that men have of telling women in private conversations that they are not interested in hearing what they have to say, put women in the position of having to stand up for their rights, on a daily, personal, ongoing basis—or trying to somehow ignore or consider 'not serious' . . . the constant subliminal information they receive about their status.[6]

Harry Brod admits that male silence in such situations is an expression of power: 'Relieving ourselves of the obligation to communicate and disclose our feelings and desires, others are forced to be inordinately attentive to us so that they can decode our muted messages, or simply not learn what we choose to keep hidden.'[7] And Kimmel, in the same volume, suggests that men are 'trained to impose our opinions on others, whether asked for or not, with an air of supreme self-confidence and aggressive self-assurance.'[8]

Yet most men are unaware of any problem, and are likely to be shocked when the relationship breaks down. Underneath rudeness about 'the wife', they may feel fond of her, and not understand why this is not enough. But, says Hite, 'How *should* we react to being with someone who, on the one hand, frequently acts emotionally distant and inaccessible, even ridiculing you or not listening – and then on the other, at times turns to you expecting love and affection, saying he loves you?' Women learn relational skills early on in their lives, and find it difficult when men do not follow the same rules. 'Listening empathetically, drawing the woman out, supporting her projects are not first priorities in most men's definition of relationships.'[9]

Hite's research also suggests that men are treating women with increasing rudeness in single relationships, and the same may be true of relations in the workplace and society generally. The code of chivalry demanded that men treat women deferentially and protectively simply because they were female. Though this accorded women some respect, it was based on inequalities of power. For some men, women have now ceased to deserve any politeness and help because they want to be equal to men. Yet kindness should hardly be dependent on the recipient admitting the superiority of the benefactor. For Hite, the end result is that

> many men are trapped, tragically, in a kind of permanent isolation and aloneness by a system which offers them 'dominance' . . . in exchange for holding back their feelings, keeping their emotional lives in check, suffering loneliness as they attempt to judge every situation 'rationally' – and wind up with no one to whom they can . . . really talk about their feelings. Eventually, they often lose the women in their lives, too, who come to resent them and withdraw emotionally and sexually.[10]

Yet it cannot be said that men simply do not know how to relate. In courtship, men often do listen empathetically, and take an interest in what women are doing. Yet, once married, many men seem to feel that the necessity for communication and listening has ended. Hite's report on *Women and Love* reflects women's interpretation of their relationships, but her study of men, and those of other researchers, bear out these findings. Few men Hite surveyed found anything to admire about women other than physical attributes; most saw women as weak and dependent, and liked them only when women were supportive, docile and nurturing. They liked marriage because it offered domestic warmth and security; very few said they enjoyed being married because they liked or loved their wife.

Ford points out that for most men there was 'an enormous gap between the dream of a wife and house of their own, and the reality of the demands and constraints of marriage, and wives with whom they couldn't communicate and who failed to understand their needs'. Most were no good at talking about emotional problems. They wanted life at home to be as smooth as possible, and therefore did not like it when their wives wanted to 'have things out'. They felt criticized and frightened of women's feelings and the need to respond to them. Men just wanted to be left alone.[11] Hite also refers to the tremendous undercurrents of anger against women that men revealed.

Clearly, the blame for domestic strife cannot be laid only at the door of men. Women can, and do, nag, manipulate and cling. They can be verbally and occasionally physically violent. The feminist critique has seen these behaviours as logical responses to the frustrations of their lives, and has perhaps been more ready to excuse women than men for unacceptable behaviour. We need to be able to understand why men have difficulties in relating to women, and not see it as indicative of inherent evil in the male species. But the crucial difference in considering male and female behaviour is that men's attitudes and actions are sanctioned by society. It is men's view of women as over-demanding in relationships and as needing to be kept in their place, which predominates in our culture – and many women accept this picture of themselves. We have seen countless representations of what it is like for men to live with women who nag constantly. But we rarely see this from women's point of view, their frustration at living with men who are emotionally distant.

Further, there is frequently economic inequality between male and female partners, which influences the way in which each sex behaves. Women's inferior position means it is they who are advised to cede to men so that harmony is maintained, to coax men out of their moodiness, and to change their own behaviour if they are in any way annoying men. Perhaps the influence of feminism means that fewer women are prepared to take this route of self-effacement, but it is still expected of them. Men may be told to try to improve their relational skills, but so often this is something they are to do *for women*. The tendency is to regard men as normal and reasonable, with women needing extra attention because they are female – and this applies in the sexual field as well as the emotional.

James Dobson, for example, suggests that women need romance because of 'genetic influences implemented by the hypothalamus region in the brain',[12] and are therefore susceptible to warmth and kindness. But warmth and kindness are essential in any friendship, and men appreciate receiving them as much as women. It is important for men to learn to talk about their feelings, and to be sensitive to the feelings of others. But they should do this as part of the process of becoming mature human beings, not just to humour the little woman. Perhaps, just as women have been encouraged to see their lack of assertion as sin, so men might accept their weakness in relationships as a sin to be forgiven and redeemed. The emotional distancing that is so many men's normal mode of relating is a travesty of what God intends for us. Veronica Zundel points out that Christian advice on male/female relationships treats them as quite different from other relationships. Yet, as she says, 'Whenever we begin to give the impression that the point of male-female relationships is radically different from the point of any other relationships, that men and women can't really be expected to achieve deep unity on the emotional or spiritual level . . . we are being . . . positively unChristian.'[13]

It is sometimes suggested that men and boys direct their emotions on to facts, games and objects, as a defence against, as well as a substitute for, intimate relationships. Yet even where their relationships with each other do focus on shared external interests, they clearly do have caring friendships which should not be underestimated. Men and boys do appear more ready than women and girls to have an intensely competitive attitude towards collecting anything from facts to stickers or stamps. They may show addictive behaviour to things such as computers, sport or work. Ironically, though this may in the end destroy their relationships and their health, important discoveries and creations may result from the ability (and opportunity) to pursue a course with such single-minded devotion.

Anne Schaef suggests that addictive behaviour of this sort stems from people's need to feel in control, 'in order to protect themselves from a universe that they perceive may overpower them'. People who are compulsive about work, sex, hobbies, accumulating money or religion are often trying to avoid the complexities of their inner lives. 'Quick-fix' religions, suggests Schaef, are those which 'avoid thoughtful prayer, meditation, and dialogue and claim to have all the answers.' The religious addict, like other addicts, loses touch with personal values, and descends into judgementalism, dishonesty and control.[14] In relationships, people move from one to the other as quickly as possible, never finding true intimacy.

Schaef identifies the Addictive System with what she has formerly called the 'White Male System'. This is not to say that all men, and only men, behave in this way, but that it is a system which has arisen out of men's experiences of the world. It is a system in which the ambiguities of life and its mixed human emotions are experienced as threatening and subjected to rigid control. Women, who raise these complex feelings in men, are feared and treated as inferior.

For Marilyn French it is 'the elevation of control into a governing principle, a god, in human life; and the identification of men with that principle', which explains male oppression of women. Men's attempt to dominate women does not bring happiness because it 'makes impossible the most essential, felicitous element in life: trusting mutual affection'. And, she says, the one who has power is trapped, for 'the dominator always belongs to the dominated ... must spend his life devising controls, silencing mechanisms, and motivations to keep the dominated in line ... is never free from the demand of the dark murmuring oppressed mass he controls.'[15] The experience of the men in Hite's research bears this out. Many of them clearly feel the need to be in control and to dominate women, yet they also express anger at the constant expectation that they should be dominant, and resent women's weakness and dependence on them. They are trapped by their own interpretations of what their relationship with women should be, and may attribute unrealistic degrees of power to women. In this sense, women have power over men at the same time that they are oppressed.

If power and control are so highly valued, they will be the main qualities ascribed to God. Brian Wren usefully explores both what control means for men, and its theological implications, in *What Language Shall I Borrow?* Feminist theologians have been critical of the tendency to understand God primarily as the all-powerful controller. Although some idea of God's transcendence is essential, when people cling to this idea of God because of their own anxieties and inadequacies, they feel threatened by the thought that God can be described in other ways. Janet Morley has observed that if there is one thing more scandalous than calling God 'She', it is calling God 'Vulnerable', as she does in *All Desires Known*.[16] Yet such a notion of God's vulnerability is at the heart of the Incarnation. God takes the risk of being misunderstood and unrecognized in Christ. And crucifixion can only happen to a God who has foregone all power and control.

What put God on the cross, says Jane Williams, was human power, and fear 'that God should not be the kind of God we want, God the King'. She continues: 'The resurrection shows us that God is free of our ideas of him and that we too can be free . . . of the need for power over one another and God.'[17] Living out the presence of God should not mean that we lord it over others, or deny the uncertainties and complexities of life. Yet so much that is written to guide men in their Christian lives emphasizes the need for them to control their passions and to be dominant in relation to women. Social and spiritual life is to be ordered in strictly hierarchical fashion, they are told; we are all the subjects of our Almighty Heavenly King, and women are subject to men as the Church is to Christ. But such a model is static, each has a fixed place and there is no chance for new discoveries about God or human capabilities.

There is a place for functional hierarchy, particularly in larger organizations, where some need to be responsible for final decisions. It does not follow that other relationships must always be ordered hierarchically. It may be said that such hierarchies are not about worth but about function, yet when power is institutionalized in one group, superior worth inevitably attaches itself to that group. The Church, especially Anglican, Catholic and Orthodox denominations, describes its leaders as servants of the servants of God, yet accords them a very high status. Diocesan Church House in Oxford has its walls dominated by huge portraits of past bishops, and it is disconcerting, not to say contradictory, to sit beneath their eye discussing God's bias to the poor and humble.

Jesus challenges his disciples not to lord it over others, or to seek power for themselves. Yet as Peter Clark observes, Christ's followers are reluctant 'to believe that God can finally be manifest in powerlessness', and in the New Testament 'we see the foundations of a rigid hierarchism being dug from the earliest days of the Church', which is still with us.[18] It is difficult to judge how much more important control and hierarchy are for men than for women, though it is often suggested that women generally prefer other ways of working. Women can operate their own hierarchies; for example, white women are guilty of racism. But the Church as a whole needs to be critical both of its established hierarchies, and of the informal ones which place clergy before laity, white before black, or men before women. We need to attack the principle that the world must necessarily be ordered hierarchically, so that one sex or the other must be dominant.

It is all too easy for women to see themselves as superior to men on a moral hierarchy, yet it is important that all the blame for society's ills is not placed on men. Women also sin, and need to change some of their patterns of thinking. Christian women know of their own capacity for sin, and know too that they cannot abandon the male half of humanity, however great the oppressiveness of the systems of patriarchy in which men are implicated. Ruether is clear that the 'systems of domination ... are "male" only in the historical and sociological sense that males have shaped and benefited from them, not in the sense that they correspond to unique, evil capacities of males that women do not share.' She points out that women's

> affirmation of their own humanity as more fundamental than their sexist conditioning demands a like affirmation of the humanity of males. Separatism ... [makes] women normative humanity and males 'defective' members of the human species. This enemy-making of males projects onto males all the human capacities for competitive relations and ego-power drives and hence denies that women too possess these capacities as part of their humanity.[19]

It is of course much easier if we can polarize the world into good and evil in this way. Life is so much less complicated when one knows one is *right*. If other people can be condemned as the enemy, we can escape the unpleasant reality that *all* of us are a complex mixture of good and bad. And it is divisive in any campaign to have to admit that the other side not only has a point, but is made up of real people with feelings. The Christian must always remember that those on the other side are people made in God's image and loved by God. I admit to finding that difficult when my own cherished beliefs are involved, but I know I should stay open to the possibility that those I disagree with may have some valuable insights into the nature of God and Christian living that I do not.

Stressing the common humanity of women and men, and insisting that women are not blameless, must not mean a softening of the feminist critique of patriarchy. Our faith may demand that we respect each other's personhood, but it also lays on us the demands of justice. It can be quite difficult to hold these two elements together when considering some of the excesses of male behaviour towards women; but the task has to be undertaken.

Chapter 7

Stormy passions

Will all the women present please cross their legs and close the gates of hell.[1]

O let me hear thee speaking
In accents clear and still,
Above the storms of passion
The murmurs of self-will.

Sex is holy, sex is sacramental, sex is what builds the church.[2]

One of the problems which exercised our church youth group when I was a teenager was this: when a Christian couple married and were on the first night of their honeymoon, should they have a time of prayer together before jumping into bed? We rather felt they ought to, but that this might take the edge off their passion. We were taught that sex within marriage was good and pleasurable. But it also came across as being very worthy and pure, quite different from the dangerous feelings we were having to keep under control lest we 'go too far'. Much Christian teaching is bedevilled by this contradiction. Sex within marriage has to be affirmed, yet passion and abandonment to pleasure seem far removed from the life of the Spirit. How does one have a fulfilling sexual relationship whilst exercising peace, goodness and self-control, and having put to death all the passions and desires of human nature (Gal. 5. 22–4)?[3] That problem may be a peculiarly Western and perhaps a Protestant one, but it is real for many people.

In some areas of the Church, more emphasis is being placed on sexuality as good, as long as it is expressed only within marriage. Though female subordination may still be part of the package, such writings at least have a more healthy attitude towards sexuality. There may also be an emphasis on the husband and wife being everything to each other, though this excludes an examination of how sexuality emerges in other relationships with friends or colleagues. The Christian critique is inadequate in many cases because no connection is made with sexuality in the world at large, other, perhaps, than to say that 'the world' has got it wrong. But it is important to take account of studies of sexuality, and in particular the feminist analysis of the sexual relations between women and men. This is something which is happening in the United States, for example in the work of Marie Fortune and Joy Bussert.

James Nelson, in *Embodiment*, offers a good critique of recent Christian theology about sexuality. He suggests there are three common attitudes towards sexuality in Christian thought. One is the idea that we can control our sexual desires through reason and will, for higher purposes. The second that sexuality has been repressed and must be reclaimed, the third that sex is unimportant, and must be laughed at as an irrational, impersonal force. But in each of these cases, sex is placed somewhere 'out there'; it is not seen as an essential part of our being bodily creatures.[4]

Our sexuality is fundamental to us as human beings, we exist as sexual beings whether or not we have active sexual relationships with others. Sexuality is the means by which we cement our most intimate relationships. It does, of course, also enable us to conceive children, but most human sexual encounters do not have this as their primary aim. Yet rather than promoting harmony between men and women, sex is often destructive of relationships, or completely divorced from them. Male sexuality in particular gets used as a weapon to demean women. Sex is treated as if it were some market commodity rather than the most intimate exchange possible between human beings. Our society operates with certain constructions of what male and female sexuality is, which only serve to deepen the gulf between the sexes.

Female sexuality is seen as essentially passive until aroused by a man. But once thoroughly aroused, it is rampant, and sexually rapacious women pose a threat to men. This is a common theme in pornographic fantasies. It is also found in women's romantic fantasies, where the heroine is awakened to desire by the hero. Yet this picture of women's sexuality does not fit the way many actually experience it. The description of women's sexuality as pervading their whole bodies may have been overdone, but it is expressed in other activities and states, such as pregnancy, birth and breast-feeding. Like men, women may move between feeling a desire to be active, and taking, and the desire to be receptive, the one who is seduced. If all women really were completely passive, lesbian sexual relationships would be an impossibility. Yet many women find it difficult to take responsibility for their own sexuality, expecting that men will always take the initiative and awaken women's desire. Like Trish in 'Strangers in the Night', they may feel too embarassed to admit to enjoying things that make them feel sexy.

It is important that women take responsibility for their own sexuality; and expect men to do the same. This means rejecting the idea that women are always responsible for men's sexual feelings, and should therefore dress and behave in such a way as to disguise their sexuality. It is not acceptable for men to argue that because a woman tries to look attractive, she is therefore asking for a sexual relationship with any or every man she meets, and must never say no. It is a common myth, perhaps especially amongst Christians who are uneasy about sexuality, that rape or unwanted sexual attention are brought about by women or girls dressing and behaving provocatively. As one woman puts it: 'I strongly feel that as Christian women it is up to us to do all we can not to lead our male neighbours (including our ministers and pastors) into temptation. Many a tragedy could be avoided, if women would behave differently and decently.'[5]

This may seem sensible at first sight. After all, it would be unfair of women to behave in a sexually provocative way with men they do not want, or who are not free to respond to them. But women can receive unwanted attention *however* they dress or behave, and men's problem seems to be with the

female sex as a whole 'radiating sex' and tempting them. Thus the 'antidote' to sexual temptation suggested in the article which gave rise to the above letter is comprehensive: 'Don't take your secretary to lunch. Don't see the opposite sex alone at night. Don't meet them in their homes. Don't sit on their beds in the hospital . . . Don't put your arms around their shoulders.'[6] Women here are seen as a constant danger to men, and the possibility that women may find men sexually disturbing is absent. This view further denies the possibility that sexuality might enrich 'non-sexual' relationships between women and men, without this being a problem. It is also naive, given that around ten per cent of the population is homosexual, to imagine that mixing only with one's own sex avoids sexual temptation. Indeed, homosexuality may be even more common in closed, same-sex organizations or groupings.

It is still difficult for women to be sexually assertive without getting a bad name. Women learn early on that 'nice girls' should not appear too enthusiastic about sex, and often absorb the belief that sex is something a man does to them, rather than part of a relationship in which they have an equal share. Women who take the lead in initiating relationships with men, or in sex itself, are seen as hard and dominating. There is still a sexual double standard which accepts that boys and men can be promiscuous, but judges women and girls much more harshly. This certainly does not mean we should advocate promiscuity amongst women for the sake of liberation. It does mean that both sexes should be judged on the same basis. In recent years, women have been encouraged to discover their own bodies. This has been helpful in terms of women's health, and it is also good if women are able to be more in tune with their sexuality. But as Segal suggests in her discussion of this trend, a concentration on a woman's own unique sexual needs 'completely submerges any notions of sexuality as a type of communication, understanding or relationship'.[7] It is reproducing what men are criticized for doing.

Yet women have always been capable of divorcing sex from relationships. Many have done so because they have never experienced sex as pleasurable, and they expect their sexual experiences to be devoid of love and tenderness. Women who are prostitutes take this even further. Critiques of prostitution may concentrate on the women's behaviour, and in the past it was they who were likely to be prosecuted rather than their clients. Yet there is a demand both for the depersonalized sexual activity they offer, and for the variety of sexual practices they will perform, which men may feel unable to do with their regular partners.[8]

Women may use sex as a way of managing men. They may trade it for favours, or accept that sex is the price they pay for being married. Hite found a great many men who believed they were buying sex when they spent money on a girl friend or wife. When asked whether they had ever used a prostitute or paid for sex, the most common reaction was that men always pay anyway: 'A prostitute is a hell of a lot more honest than the domestic prostitutes that go under the label as wives, at least you get what you pay for.'[9] Women may also use sex as a way of defusing anger and violence. They may give sex to men in the same way that they give sweets to children – to shut them up and keep them happy. It may be, for many women, simply another way in which they are expected selflessly to service men's needs. Men in their turn may be aware of this attitude and find it difficult. To know that the woman they love is merely putting up with sexual intercourse as a duty is painful for them. This too is clear from Hite's work, and such a reaction belies the idea that men are not emotionally involved in their sexual encounters.

There is a curious gap between the image of aggressive, confident male sexuality which predominates in our culture, and the reality of men's experience. Men may even talk in the confident language of the former when at heart they feel vulnerable and want intimate relationships. Many of the men Anna Ford interviewed saw sex as 'pure fun which fulfilled a strong need, and the pleasure was unrelated to the need for a profound relationship, or even to knowing the person concerned. The pleasure was often short-lived.' As one seventeen-year-old boy put it, 'You're not a bloke until you've done it. It's got to be done.' But her lasting impression was 'of men's deepdown confusion over emotional involvement with another person'. They wanted to please and perform well, were uncertain what women wanted, but were not prepared to discuss it, even with those they loved. 'Huge communication gaps yawned in this area of men's lives. Vulnerable, afraid of appearing inadequate, determined to keep their outward image untarnished, most did what they thought was expected of them, as best they could.'[10]

It is easy to see how men might be trapped by the common view of male sexuality as being solely about 'performance, penetration, conquest'.[11] Marie Fortune describes male sexuality as including: a desire that its object be 'innocent', i.e. powerless, passive, subordinate, a need to objectify the other to avoid intimacy, a lack of regard for the other as an autonomous person, an inability to find erotic/emotional pleasure with an equal.[12] It is, moreover, aggressive. If Fortune's analysis of how male sexuality is constructed in our society is right, it is a terrible indictment. Yet we seem to accept that that is how men are: in the grip of uncontrollable urges, taking sex by violence if the urge is over-strong, unable to relate emotionally to women.

Much popular Christian material which talks about male sexuality gives this picture, and there is little public questioning of whether this is what it is really like. It is either accepted as a fact of life, or even made a virtue. The general idea is that God has made men performance-orientated (in sex as in other things), and women interested in people. But since men are supposed to cherish their wives, they will try to be romantic some of the time. Plattner advocates this. He says it is hard for husbands to accept that women want to feel understood and appreciated, but thinks if men try, they may in the end find this difference in women delightful.[13] The key problem for men is lust, and the debate in *Leadership Today* referred to earlier is a good example of how it is to be tackled. Principally, men are to avoid women, who are inherently dangerous. Taylor advises Christian men to keep their distance from women, lest it lead to disaster: 'The married Christian worker who is alert to the perils which beset him and is self-disciplined always in look and word and action will not ignite fires which he will have to fight feverishly to put out.'[14]

Taylor's picture is of men desperately trying to repress their sexuality, but this attitude only makes the problem worse. Marriage is seen as the only legitimate outlet for turbulent sexual feelings, though this only helps heterosexual men. And women have to be respected and are not expected to be passionate. Men who have grown up dividing women into two camps, good mothers and 'loose women', may find it difficult to be adventurous and passionate with their own wives and the mothers of their children, and this may be one reason why so many have affairs outside marriage. The Christian man is constantly having to sublimate his natural masculine sexuality, and to try to be patient, tender and restrained out of love for God and woman. Not surprisingly, this is a recipe for frustration. Yet the view that it is always a struggle to control the male sexual drive is widespread. It does, of course, contradict the other common picture of the male sex as logical, rational and in control. But by separating off their sexuality from the rest of themselves, men can maintain the appearance of superiority.

Boys learn very early that their sexual drive cannot be controlled, and most experiment with sexuality free from any idea that they should exercise restraint or responsibility. Most of the men in Ford's book did not see themselves as naturally monogamous; the male sex drive was thought to be too strong. The fact that male homosexuals tend to be promiscuous is sometimes thought to indicate that this is how men 'naturally' behave if left to themselves. On the other hand, society and Church offer no publicly sanctioned alternative for those who practise homosexuality.

Some men do react against being seen as 'only interested in one thing', for they feel this denies the other parts of their personality. The idea that male sexuality is nothing to do with the rest of men's existence must be challenged. For it is a very low view both of sexuality and of men to accept that they naturally engage in sex without noticing their partner, or getting emotionally involved. Though it has been a strand of

73

Christian teaching in the past to despise sexuality, most Christians today would wish to affirm it as something that is central to our humanity and our relationships. God presumably does not intend men to treat it as just another human appetite.

But equally, it does not help to divide sex into pure and impure forms, as Christians so often do. One writer distinguishes between 'sexuality' and 'eros'. Sexuality is self-centred, and wants the satisfaction of lust and sensual desire. Because it carries out the task of procreation, it is willed by God but 'there is something unnatural about it when it is excited and experienced purely for its own sake.' Eros, on the other hand, is concerned with the other. It brings out grace, kindness, charm and delicacy in women, chivalry, courage, gentlemanly behaviour and attentiveness in men. It enables people to give themselves to each other. The problem can then be defined as men confusing eros and sexuality. Young men, says Bovet, need to be educated beyond sex and up to eros. 'They need to be shown that the object of their main interest – a woman's body – though not in itself by any means evil or unimportant, is far less interesting than is a woman as a whole person: body, mind and spirit.'[15]

The tendency is to continue the same dualistic mode of thought which makes particular virtues masculine or feminine, and asserts that we therefore need to put both sexes together to get the whole picture. With sexuality, men are seen as having the sensual passion, whilst women have tenderness and love. But it does not work when the two come together, because these attributes are experienced as opposites. We need a way of thought which does not just see individuals as holding masculine and feminine qualities side by side, but sees how these characteristics weave into one another. Rousseau and Gallagher explore this, pointing out that the separation of passion from tenderness is inappropriate: 'To many people's minds, sexual passion is rough and violent, a selfish, brute force . . . But passion and violence don't have to go together. Passion and vigorous, energetic activity – yes, but passionate people can also be tender, kind, gentle, loving. Passion can be a lusty affection.'[16]

Because God and religion have been associated with the 'feminine' list of attributes, God is often placed in opposition to sex and passion too. Christians may plead to hear God's 'clear and still' accents 'above the storms of passion' – it's noticable how many hymns reflect this view. The evangelist who describes his battle with lust writes: 'I began to view sex as another of God's mistakes, like tornados and earthquakes. In the final analysis it only caused misery. Without it, I could conceive of becoming pure and godly ... With sex, any spiritual development seemed hopelessly unattainable.'[17]

That theme of moving on from sensuality to a purer mode is a common one, but it still leaves sexuality unconnected with the rest of life. Men are left having to fight a continuing battle to prevent their passions taking over. Rousseau and Gallagher, though they rather overstate the case, are clear that sexual passion is vital in marriage. Their thesis that 'passion gives parents an exquisite gentleness with each other and with their children' has not, as far as I am aware, been subject to research. But they are right to be critical of 'bridled sex, passion that is inhibited by false fears and a dutiful approach to life'. For them, sexual passion is a Christian sacrament: 'People who are their own persons, in control, self-possessed, cannot symbolize a God of three persons who are totally, passionately, ecstatically poured forth to each other.'[18]

Studies of sexuality do find differences in the sexual responses of men and women, and I am not suggesting that male and female sexuality are identical. However, with sexual, as with other differences between the sexes, a number of responses are possible. It is necessary to point out that we can only generalize about female and male sexuality, and there will be many individuals who do not fit the pattern. Moreover, sexuality is experienced differently at different stages of life. We can also choose whether to encourage 'natural' differences or act to reduce their influence. But in any case, Hite's research questions many of our assumptions. For example, she shows that women can become aroused very quickly given the right kind of stimulation, and that men enjoy a whole range of sexual intimacy as well as, or in place of, intercourse.

Hite is deeply critical of the way that sex is equated with intercourse and the male orgasm, with woman's role being to help the man along. Sex then finishes when the man finishes, and the woman's needs are not treated with equal seriousness. This not only leads to frustration for many women, but puts pressure on men. Though intercourse makes a man feel a man ('You're not a bloke till you've done it'), many men are ambivalent about the fact that the success of the whole thing depends on their performance. We are so used to this model that it is difficult to think there might be other approaches. But Hite shows that things can be different. She speaks of the more diffuse aspects to men's sexuality and sensuality, and the spontaneous enthusiasm men had for other kinds of sexual intimacy. One of the reasons they enjoyed intercourse was that it made them feel loved and accepted; they did not simply see it as a means to a quick orgasm.[19]

It would help if both sexes were able to share more closely their confused, contradictory feelings about sexuality and relationships. Women have sometimes found it difficult to acknowledge the strength of their sexual feelings, and that may be particularly the case for Christians. Men have felt they must live up to the image of the male as sexual expert, and have been reluctant to admit that emotional involvement is important to them, because this threatens their image of invulnerability. As Ingham says, 'Boys have few opportunities to express any ambivalence they may feel about sexual intimacy . . . From the moment they discover what "it" is all about, they must never appear reluctant or unwilling to indulge once given the opportunity.'[20] The pressure on men to perform leads to fears of inadequacy and being rejected. And where men always take the lead, they do not know what it is to feel sexually desirable themselves.

All of this must be handled within the context of emotional involvement, for whether men find it easy to express their feelings or not, they do have feelings! Women are supposed to be more interested in love and romance, but this is a moot point. David Lodge gives a clever portrayal, in his book *Nice Work*,[21] of the hard-headed male industrialist who listens to sentimental romantic music in his car and believes himself in love after one sexual encounter. In poetry, pop songs, novels, television, men are frequently pouring out passionate feelings of love and vulnerability. Presumably this reflects male experience rather than being put on only for the sake of women. It may fade later in the relationship, but in courtship, men and boys are often just as romantic as women. Indeed, it may be that men are more likely to be blinded by love than are women, who often have a rather pragmatic view of their relationships.

However, there is a mass market amongst women for romantic novels and stories. In romantic literature, emotionally distant and callous men become tender through the love of a good and pure woman. It is this fantasy that a woman can awaken a man's tender heart (whilst he awakens her sexuality) which makes romance an attractive genre for many women, even committed feminists. Yet, as Coward points out,

> The qualities which make these men so desirable are . . . the qualities which feminists have chosen to ridicule: power (the desire to dominate others); privilege (the exploitation of others); emotional distance (the inability to communicate); and singular love for the heroine (the inability to relate to anyone other than the sexual partner).[22]

In a perceptive paper, Morgan argues that women have been conditioned to be aroused by male dominance, rather than by the male body or men's personal qualities. Yet women may feel alienated from themselves when they are attracted by male dominance, because they cannot constantly submit to it without losing their self respect. Morgan writes that a man may genuinely not understand why his chivalric deference and protectiveness may move a woman sexually, but do not make her feel affirmed as a person.[23] It is because they believe there is no escape from male dominance in heterosexual relationships that some feminists advocate lesbianism as the only kind of sexuality that affirms women.[24]

Morgan's analysis may help to explain the ambivalent feelings many women have about the so-called 'New Man'. Whilst wanting to encourage men to be caring and show their feelings, women tend to be scornful of wimps. They may rationalize that attitude by saying that they want both women and men to have some strength of character, but it is probably more complex than that. For the sake of more mature and fulfilling relationships which do not alienate either men or women from themselves, we must begin to find new models of what it means to be a man. Women will need to look again at the complexities of their desire, and to learn to respect men who do not fit in with the present stereotype of masculinity.

It is clear that both sexes suffer from confused and ambivalent feelings about their sexuality. The persistence with which people enter sexual relationships indicates that something good is expected from them; but the encounters are often unsatisfactory. Some Christians would argue that the reason for dissatisfaction is that so many sexual relationships take place outside marriage, and because they are short-lived, do not give a couple a chance to build up understanding. This may be the case, but sex can be unsatisfactory in committed Christian marriages as well. Part of the reason for this is that we all grow up in a culture which defines sexuality in particular ways, and lays particular expectations upon us. Those who wish to affirm a positive Christian sexuality expressed through the marriage relationship, still need to take account of the culture in which it must be lived out.

Chapter 8

A cheap way to buy
a woman

Maybe most men who view pornography just want the raw sex, sort of like going to a prostitute, without all the 'expense' of emotional involvement. Or maybe they just want to feel like men, buying it and looking at it. It's a cheap way to buy a woman.[1]

On the macabre cannibalism of female praying mantises:
When they mate, the male cautiously creeps up on the female, mounts her, and copulates. If the female gets the chance, she will eat him, beginning by biting his head off, either as the male is approaching, or immediately after he mounts, or after they separate. It might seem most sensible for her to wait until copulation is over before she starts to eat him. But the loss of the head does not seem to throw the rest of the male's body off its sexual stride. Indeed, since the insect head is the seat of some inhibitory nerve centres, it is possible that the female improves the male's sexual performance by eating his head.[2]

When I have read Richard Dawkins' story of female praying mantises to both mixed and women's groups, it is generally received with amusement. But I have then gone on to ask how the group would react to a different scenario, of an audience listening to a man tell of a species where the female's sexual performance is improved by her head being bitten off before copulation. Such a story would carry a different meaning. It would conjure up reminders of sexual violence against women, of men thinking women at their best when silent, of pornographic pictures that cut off the woman's face and head.

If it was simply the case that men and women experienced difficulties in their sexual relationships with each other, it would be serious enough. But presumably for people who liked or loved each other, it would be possible to work these problems out together. The difficulty in the present situation is that sexual relationships are played out against a backcloth of sexual violence and hostility between the sexes. We live in a society where large numbers of women are subjected to rape and sexual assault. Pornography is booming, and its images getting more violent and lurid. Even within our intimate relationships, sex is used as a weapon, and sexual partners are treated with contempt. Such problems are not resolved by individual couples being more thoughtful. Destructive attitudes towards sexuality are entrenched deep within society, and it is hard to see how to begin to tackle them.

In order to oppose something effectively, it is necessary to have a common consensus that it is wrong. A major difficulty in the area of pornography and sexual violence is that many people do not regard it as a problem. Whilst rapists are shunned in prisons by other men, there is a strong body of popular opinion which suggests that women enjoy the experience of rape, or precipitate the attack by their own provocative behaviour. Men who read pornography may say, 'What is wrong with enjoying looking at pictures of pretty girls?' Or of harder porn, that it stops 'perverts' actually doing anything about their fantasies. Yet as Posy Simmonds shows, heterosexual men at least are likely to be acutely uncomfortable at the sight of naked male pin-ups, or if they feel they are being looked at as sex objects. Christians have generally agreed that pornography is wrong, though they have been ambivalent about sexual violence. Acceptance of women's subordination within marriage can make it difficult for Christians to appreciate non-consensual (not-mutually-desired) sex as a problem.

It is important to establish the base from which one looks at pornography. Fortune states that there are two reactions to pornography. One is that sex itself is 'bad', and since porn equals sex, therefore porn is bad. The other reaction says that sex is good, and since porn equals sex, porn is good. Christians are likely to be identified with the first category, though as the last chapter showed, it is sexual passion which makes many

Christians uncomfortable, rather than the existence of sex itself. Sex can be affirmed as God's creation, as long as it is gentle and pure. Pornography may be seen as bad because it is sexually arousing, and threatens the institution of marriage by exposing young men to strong sexual stimulation.[3] But pornography is not bad because it is about sex. It is the particular way in which sex is portrayed that makes it offensive. Fortune defines porn as 'sexually explicit material which portrays abuse, violence, and degradation for the purpose of arousal and entertainment'. She distinguishes this from the erotic, sexual material which may or may not be explicit, used for arousal and entertainment, but not involving violence.[4]

Pornography is notoriously difficult to define. For some, it is any material which is sexually stimulating, for others it may depend on the intention of the producer. Fortune's definition raises two major questions. Firstly, how is it possible in practice to label what is porn and what is erotica? Susanne Kappeler argues convincingly that the problem is the way women are viewed, and that the same way of seeing them underlies both kinds of material, as well as being widespread in society. She suggests that there is a 'pornographic structure of representation' under which women are consistently seen as objects, whilst men are the subjects who look and act. And this is 'a commonplace of art and literature as well as of conventional pornography'. There will be no consensus that pornography is wrong because it objectifies and degrades women, if that way of seeing women is the norm for the culture. Rather than criticizing porn and defending erotic art, Kappeler suggests that 'responsibility for the dominant modes of representation . . . needs to be sought in "responsible" art and "high" culture, rather than in its waste products.'[5]

And secondly, there is the argument that the display of women's bodies for arousal and entertainment itself constitutes violence against women. The 'mild' porn magazine *Hustler* showed a woman lying on her back, legs open, while a man bored into her vagina with a pile driver. Hard core magazines have included pictures of breasts being crushed in vices, exploding vaginas packed with hand grenades, women having intercourse with pigs and dogs. There are close-ups of women's bodies bound, gagged and hung.[6] I have no wish to dwell on such images, but we need to know what we are talking about. Soft porn may be less likely to include violent images, but regardless of whether abuse is shown, or whether it causes actual assaults, many women find it demeaning and upsetting. This was borne out by a survey in *Cosmopolitan* magazine in 1990. One might expect readers of that magazine to be more permissive about sexuality and pornography than women in general. Yet 91 per cent found adult/men's magazines offensive.[7]

Earlier feminist opposition to porn arose out of the belief that it was linked to actual assaults. In Robin Morgan's well-known phrase, 'pornography is the theory, rape is the practice.' This tended to lead to the bandying of statistics, which proved points for both sides but did not lead to a consensus. There does seem to be a link between some sexual assaults and the use of pornography; but many users of porn do not go on to commit offences. Nonetheless, pornography may legitimate the fantasies which lead to actual assault, and provide a model for putting these into action. Porn is designed to make people feel and behave differently – they are supposed to be aroused and want sex after reading or viewing it. We might therefore expect violent porn to have some effect on attitudes, and Mike Baxter suggests that this is what happens:

> The weight of evidence is accumulating that intensive exposure to soft-core pornography desensitizes men's attitude to rape, increases sexual callousness and shifts their perferences towards hard-core pornography. . . Exposure to violent pornography increases men's acceptance of rape myths and of violence against women.[8]

The Campaign against Pornography and Censorship speaks of legislating against pornography on the grounds that it perpetuates sex discrimination and is an incitement to sexual hatred and violence.[9] This may be a more helpful way of viewing it, since it opposes porn as an infringement of women's rights rather than because it is about sexuality. However, this does need to be linked in some way with the wider context of how women are viewed in society.

It should also be remembered that it is real women who are filmed and photographed, and this can involve violence and coercion. Women may be driven into pornography and prostitution by economies which offer few other choices. Some research suggests that 90 per cent of prostitutes or pornographic models were abused as children, and if the percentage is anything like as high as that, then pornography is built on the exploitation of those who are already vulnerable.[10]

Pornography is supposed to be sexy and enjoyable, and some women share this feeling about it. Many others feel pressured by men into looking at it in magazines or on video. One of the worrying aspects of the *Cosmopolitan* survey was that more than a third of respondents had first had contact with porn whilst under the age of twelve, and two-thirds of them under the age of sixteen. This included seeing illegal pornography. Though 81 per cent of them saw porn frequently or occasionally, two-thirds of them did not choose to do so. They might go along with a partner who wanted to use it with them, but over half of them had reservations about it. Whilst they found it arousing, they also felt negative, disgusted, guilty, and offended. Pornography *is* sexually stimulating; after all, that is what it is designed to be. Though aimed at men, it is likely to stir up sexual feelings in women even if it also leaves them feeling dirty and alienated. Supporters of pornography suggest that these negative feelings arise from negative feelings about sex itself. But it is quite reasonable for women to feel upset at the objectification and abuse of women in porn, whilst being positive about sexuality in general. The *Cosmopolitan* readers were clear that they liked erotic material which showed reciprocal sex, rather than sex as something done to women by men.

Experiments have been tried with explicit pornography for women. Lesbian pornography is growing, which sometimes includes sado-masochistic themes, and its use is vigorously defended by some feminists.[11] Pornography for heterosexual women has not proved successful. The naked male body is more likely to arouse women's curiosity and amusement, than their desire. A fairly recent genre is that of the 'sex-busters' written by and for women. These are read widely, and are explicit in their descriptions of sexual encounters. Such books might be regarded as pornographic for this reason, but they are not usually as exploitative of women or men. Women have a much more active sexuality in them, though there is a danger of copying the tendency criticized in men, to separate sex from relationships. Romantic fiction for women is highly popular, and though the sexuality may be less explicit, the story line may not be so very dissimilar from that of pornography, with the masterful male awakening female desire.

Pornography is big business, and exists to make money – some £500 million a year in the United Kingdom and $10 billion in the United States.[12] As with drugs, the market is unlimited, since addicts crave ever new products to give them kicks. Manufacturers may encourage humanitarian-sounding justifications of their product: soft porn helps preserve marriage by improving a couple's sex life, or helps boys and men who are seeking information about sex. But it is questionable whether the perpetuation of porn's images of women encourages healthy mutual relationships, or provides very accurate information. The difficulty is partly that many people are unhappy about public sex education, and Christians have often been in the forefront of campaigns to limit its form and content. Yet it can be argued that we have a society in which many people, especially the young, are profoundly ignorant about sex. Lee, in her fascinating study of sex education in schools, reports that over 80 per cent of teenagers she met had had no sex education at home, and only 1 per cent believed that what they had received was meaningful.[13]

Pornography may also be justified as sexually liberating, and this is a main reason why it has burgeoned over the last thirty years. Interestingly, one result of the upheavals in Eastern Europe has been a growth in pornography and sex shops.

People raised in a sexually prudish culture have welcomed porn as something liberating. A reporter told of how whole families (of adults) were visiting sex shops and coming out with armfuls of material, and how one pornographer was receiving letters of thanks from satisfied customers: 'We cried, the material was so beautiful,' said one.[14] But it must be repeated that, whilst material which helps people enjoy their sexuality in committed relationships is acceptable, the predominant message of porn is destructive. And we might wish to be suspicious about the pornographers and sex shop owners' humanitarian justifications of their product, since their main interest is in opening up new markets for profit. We may also be told that since women now produce pornography, and men are sometimes treated as objects, there can be no complaint. But if it is wrong to treat women as objects, it cannot be right to do the same for men.

There is little alternative for those who want to explore their sexual feelings. Our society lacks a strong tradition of erotica: pictures, films or writings which are not exploitative. Some Christians will question whether any such representation of sex is necessary, arguing that it is a private matter between husband and wife. Yet we need some public exploration of sexual relationships if we are to grow in them. We need both practical knowledge and an understanding of the emotional and spiritual significance of sex. The Song of Songs perhaps points the way forward in suggesting that human sexual love can be described and celebrated openly, in a way which is not offensive.

A further question is whether fantasy should play a part in a positive Christian view of sexuality, and if so, what it might look like. Rousseau and Gallagher do not spell out in detail what they mean, but believe that 'steady and deliberate sexual fantasizing is an important part of cultivating the intimacy that is our sacramental symbol.'[15] And Julie Reeves, following a tendency for evangelical Christians to be more positive about sexuality, suggests Christians should act on sexual fantasies with their spouses.[16] If sex is an adult form of play, it may seem quite harmless for people to have, and perhaps want to act out, fantasies. But we are creatures of our culture, and therefore our fantasies are not necessarily healthy. Any fantasy which involves someone other than the spouse might seem to go against Jesus' statement that someone who looks on another with lust has already committed adultery in their heart (Matt. 5.27–28),[17] and some have applied this to spouses as well. Both sexes may have masochistic feelings, such that women may fantasize rape, or men desire to be bound.

It has been suggested that both sexes respond to pornographic material because it represents a rejection of and hatred for the female body which correspond with some of our infantile feelings. But that still raises the question as to whether it is healthy to indulge such fantasies, or whether we should be trying to escape them. Does anything go in the private lives of a couple, or should fantasies be checked out for ideological and theological soundness? That might rather spoil sexual spontanteity!

Pornography is sometimes defended as being of use in therapy with sex offenders or those with sexual problems. Yet if pornography is accepted as an abuse of women, it cannot be ethically right to encourage its use. There must be alternative ways of helping people to resolve their difficulties or alter their behaviour. Non-exploitative, erotic material might be a healthier way of easing sexual repression, for example. If that is not satisfactory, it suggests that pornography provides another dimension, and that would seem to be that it allows men to assert their power over women. Moreover, pornography generally assumes the viewpoint of the white male, and can be blatantly racist.[18] Standard pornographic material, openly available in newsagents, includes women being beaten and humiliated, schoolgirls stripped and whipped—and because child porn is illegal, adult women with their pubic hair shaved are posed to look like little girls. These magazines display an obsessive fixation on women's open genitals and anuses, photographed close up, and posed to appear gaping, inviting sexual access. More extreme forms of pornography include bestiality, paedophilia, and in so-called 'snuff' movies, women or children may actually be killed on screen. These are not about sexuality, but about hatred and power. Women here are subdued and controlled by men.[19]

It is no accident that pornography should grow at a time when women are asserting their right to be treated equally. Pornography gives reassurance to men who feel threatened by women, and want to feel they are still in control. Hite shows how many men think of sex as a weapon, and fantasize raping a woman to put her in her place. Pornography enables men to feel power over women, and this is one reason why they overwhelmingly prefer porn in which a man is not present.[20] Segal suggests that pornography is 'a compensatory expression of men's *declining* power', rather than, as some other feminists have seen it, a means by which men exert their power over women: 'It serves to expose not imperial strength but pathetic weakness—a gargantuan need for reassurance that, at least in fantasy, women can remain eternally objects for men to use and abuse at will.' She quotes Andy Moye's view that porn works because it denies the complications and anxieties of sexuality for men: 'It is in the space between this anxiety and the fantasy realm of a perfect sexual world that pornography achieves its power.'[21]

Yet the sexual realm constructed in pornography is far from perfect. The dissatisfactions men express with their sex lives centre precisely on the consequences of being a man in the pornographic mode: always having to initiate sex, having to perform, being responsible for women's sexual responses. And it denies men's need and desire for intimacy, taking away any emotional or spiritual significance from sex. As Coward points out, pornographic images 'feed a belief that men have depersonalized sexual needs, like sleeping or going to the lavatory. Pornography . . . suggests that women's bodies are available to meet those needs.' And the pleasure men get from it, even if it is fantasy, nonetheless seems 'conditional on feeling power to use women's bodies'.[22]

Porn is under attack from several directions. Though the standpoints of the feminists and the Christians who are most vocal in their opposition are different, they are beginning to form an influential lobby. It is important to oppose pornography from a point of view which affirms sex as part of God's good creation, and which offers something positive in place of the current sexual ethic. Porn is contrary to the gospel because it objectifies and abuses women, and depersonalizes sex, not because anything that is sexually arousing is wrong. And any opposition to it must go alongside a radical critique of anything which denigrates women, including behaviour in the Church itself. Susan Griffin outlines the links between the pornographic mind and the teachings of the Church, saying that the pornographer 'reduces a woman to a mere thing, to an entirely material object without a soul', and the Judeo-Christian culture offers the same ethos.[23] Even if we would want to challenge the bluntness of her assertion, the point needs taking on. It can be no part of the Christian vision to campaign for a society in which pornography is eliminated, but women continue to be treated as subordinate to men.

Arguments continue about whether censorship is the best method of opposition. It raises difficult questions about the definition of pornography, and individual rights. Clearly, banning all pornography would merely drive it underground, and make it even more lucrative for the porn business. Yet it would help to reduce the amount publicly available. The display of pornography on newsagents' shelves gives the message that it is an acceptable 'general interest', equivalent to yachting or computing. A society which really believed that women and men were equal would long ago have ceased to legitimate material that abuses women, by having it so openly available. The 'Off the Shelf' campaign started at the end of the 1980s aims to stop large chains of newsagents selling porn, and there has also been a campaign only to support shops which do not stock it. This may be a good way forward, in that it is using the power of consumer choice rather than the law. But the major issue is that we live in a culture in which sexuality is seen in such a sterile, depersonalized way.

Carol Lee is fiercely critical of the idea that we live in a sexually permissive age. Her experience of working with young teenagers indicates they have very little idea that sexual experience can involve tenderness and joy. Girls tend to have romantic and idealized notions about sex which are often shattered by the reality of their first sexual encounters with boys. Lee comments that hearing sex and contraception discussed frankly actually puts them off rather than encouraging them to experiment. Simply giving them the biological facts to store until they get married, as some suggest, fails to help young people to understand the complexity of sexuality and relationships. It may encourage them to split sex and relationships in precisely the way I have criticized. The Family Planning Association policy statement which Lee quotes is more holistic. It says that 'sexuality is an inseparable part of every person and should be accepted as one aspect of the total human experience'; that 'all individuals should be concerned with other people as well as themselves', and that 'individuals should be responsible for their actions'.

Lee also notes the harsh language which both boys and girls use when talking about sex, which makes them seem falsely knowledgable about it. She describes them as 'prisoners of their words, which were as injurious as blunt instruments in dulling their ability to experience what their words could not describe. . . . If tenderness is imprisoned by language, so brutality is encouraged by it.'[24] In the absence of sex education in the home, and the limited way it is taught in schools, pornography is a key source of information, particularly for teenage boys. And it provides much of the brutal language and imagery with which they express their sexuality.

Christian critiques of pornography tend to be inadequate because they fail to set it in its context. A proper critique will question why male sexuality is expressed in this violent and woman-hating form. Christians often object to pornography for the same reasons they object to other things which they see as symptoms of the 'permissive society' – employed mothers, divorce, teenage delinquency. A Vatican statement on pornography and violence in the media pointed out that they 'debase sexuality, corrode human relationships, exploit individuals – especially women and young people – undermine marriage and family life, foster anti-social behaviour and weaken the moral fibre of society.' It called for higher moral standards from parents and in schools, and sound laws.[25] But surely the question we should be asking is why we as a society legitimate pernicious material which celebrates the denigration of women.

Helena Terry picks up this idea in her analysis of Christian responses to porn. She notes Catherwood's case in the 1972 Longford report which, like the Williams report, 'understands porn as a causal phenomenon which only affects the position of women by the extent of its distribution, rather than a depravity and violence against women in itself'. Catherwood implies that it is men who are dehumanized when women are turned into objects, for men are led into lust. But, says Terry, we need an approach which focuses on the degradation of women.[26] It is true that men are harmed by pornography, but this is not because it gives them more occasion for lust. Pornography is harmful because it is a terrible way for men to treat other human beings, and because it encourages men in distorted views of women and sexuality. But it must be repeated that it is not only pornography that does this. Christian men who see male sexuality as consisting of scarcely controllable urges which make them automatically see girls and women as sexual objects, are buying into the same view of the world.

Kappeler is deeply critical of the idea that a man using pornography is not actually doing anything, and that it makes no difference to his behaviour in 'real life'. The viewer *is* doing something, she says, watching and masturbating. And in the real world men are continuing to see women, whether known or unknown, in this way, as objects of their pleasure. Kappeler continues:

> The fundamental problem at the root of men's behaviour in the world, including sexual assault, rape, wife battering, sexual harassment, keeping women in the home and in unequal opportunities and conditions, treating them as objects for conquest and protection—the root problem behind the reality of men's relations with women, is the way men see women, is Seeing.[27]

Pornography is a serious problem, but it does not exist in isolation. The pornographic mind expresses itself wherever men assume the right to buy women, or control their lives, wherever women are subordinated to men.

91

· Chapter 9 ·

Sexual violence

It is a shocking thing to hear a woman say that . . . she will not be raped even by her husband. Such an attitude would be impossible in any woman to whom loving and giving were synonymous.[1]

Sex is the weapon of rape, not the reason.[2]

Sexual violence is a great cause of concern amongst women, and fear of it influences their behaviour. Attacks on women and children make headline news, but neither the media nor women themselves make much of the fact that it is *men* who are the danger. In our private relationships, it is possible to say that women also act badly towards men, but in the public sphere it is overwhelmingly *men* who harass and assault women sexually. That fact makes most of us acutely uncomfortable, women as well as men, yet unless we state the problem for what it is, we will not be able to tackle it.

Sexual violence tends to be seen in isolation as the act of a few perverted sex-monsters. But we have to see its connection with more widespread male behaviour towards women. At its least serious, this includes remarks in the street. On some occasions, women do not mind being remarked on, either because they have set out to look attractive, or because they know they look a mess and are amused. At other times, the comments make them feel acutely uncomfortable, as if they have accidentally strayed into someone else's territory (as perhaps they have), or as if their personal space has been intruded into. I cannot be the only woman who has taken the long route home to avoid having to go back past a group of men who have shouted comments at me.

Sexual harassment covers a range of behaviour from

personal comments to touching and even assault. It can be difficult to define exactly, because it is not the act but the way it is experienced which marks it as harassment. It is unwanted behaviour which is deliberately intrusive, and which has sexual overtones. Much of the touching, flirting and joking that goes on between the sexes is not sexual harassment, because it is mutual. Nor does accidental physical contact come under the heading. It is at its most problematic where there is an unequal power relation between harasser and victim, so that the victim cannot deal with it. It takes away the ability to control intimate contact. And women are much less likely than men to be in a position to force sexual attentions on men.

Several men have commented to me that they are confused, unsure what they can and can't do and say to women. They find it difficult to accept that it is the way a woman experiences an action which defines it as sexual harassment. But they should not expect there to be a single way of treating all women, any more than there is a single way of treating all men. We are required to have some sensitivity to the different personalities of the individuals we meet, and not everyone is easy to relate to. Men do need to be aware of the unequal relations between the sexes, which make it difficult for women to object to male behaviour. But those men who are clear that they do not wish to dominate women, and who try to treat them like human beings, are not likely to go too far wrong.

Male harassment of women is often talked about as if it arose purely from the desire to establish sexual contact, but this is not the case. Wise and Stanley report the experience of a six-foot tall, forty-three-year-old female marathon runner who was harassed by small boys and male youths, touching and shouting at her.[3] I have had similar experiences, and a friend was kicked by a boy as she ran past. The motivation here is not sexual but a reaction against women who step out of line and an attempt to reassert male superiority.

What these incidents of harassment share with more recognized forms of sexual violence is that, as Kelly points out, all are 'unwanted intrusions into women's personal space which transform routine and/or potentially pleasurable activities (for example, a walk in the park, a quiet evening at home, a long train journey) into unpleasant, upsetting, disturbing and often threatening experiences.'[4] Women may feel they should not be affected, or others may suggest that only the repressed or neurotic woman will be upset. When I was an undergraduate at Durham University, we used to joke about the possible effect on serious-minded Christian women of being confronted by the Prebends Flasher. Yet women's feelings of violation in such circumstances are common human reactions to intrusion. For example, those whose homes are burgled without any damage being done, and only easily replaceable items stolen, are nevertheless likely to feel very upset. Victims may feel assaulted, and no longer safe, and may take a long time to get over it.

Sexual violence is not only found in the obvious abuses of rape and battering, but lies behind a range of male behaviours. These include flashing and obscene phone-calls, which

> enact very similar assumptions about male sexuality and women's relation to it. . . . They say that men need and feel entitled to have, unrestricted sexual access to women, even – sometimes especially – against women's will . . . that man's sexuality is aggressive, predatory.

Both rape and flashing are 'acts which men do in order to reassure themselves of their power and potency; both include as a crucial factor in that reassurance, the fear and humiliation of the female victims.'[5] Men may also direct sexual violence and harassment towards other men, perhaps particularly towards boys or men who are 'feminized' by being in inferior positions. The aim here too seems to be to humiliate the victim.

It may be worth noting that sado-masochistic practices pick up on the desire of some men and women to be sexually violent with one another. Those who defend s/m see it as a safe, ritualized form of mutual pain and pleasure. There has been some debate about this within feminism, particularly as some lesbians have defended their right to be involved in sado-masochism. Others have questioned whether such desires are any more healthy when they take place between two women than between a woman and a man.[6]

It is difficult to know to what extent there is a direct causal relationship between pornography and sexual violence, since sexual violence exists apart from porn, and most porn readers do not assault women. Yet when the two are placed side by side, it is clear that they share a common root in men's fear of, and need to exert power over, women. Sex and violence are frequently spoken of in the same breath, and male sexuality is in many cases seen as synonymous with coercion and violence. For some men (and a few women), violence and abuse are sexually arousing. In many other cases, sexual activity is expected to involve male dominance and some coercion. Both romantic novels and some Christian material advocating male 'headship' and female subordination reinforce this view.

Yet however intertwined the two have become, we need to insist that they do not belong together. As well as rethinking attitudes towards sexuality, this means ceasing to interpret such offences as rape purely as sex crimes. In most cases, sexual violence emerges out of anger, aggression and the desire to dominate, not out of sexual attraction. Most men in Hite's report said they had never raped a woman, but could want to under certain conditions, usually connected with feelings of anger over rejection, or wanting to teach women a lesson.[7] The conventional picture is of the over-sexed male either with no sexual outlet or who is provoked by a woman. For example, a judge told a man who repeatedly and viciously raped a deaf and dumb woman, 'It is clear that when you drink too much you find it difficult to control your sexual urges.'[8] But the majority of rapists are sexually active with wives or partners when they rape, and they are not particular about the attractiveness of the victim. In any case, it would be much easier for them to deal with their arousal through masturbation than through rape. It is important to grasp the fact that rape is an act of violence, yet not to lose sight of its sexual nature. This is partly because we need to keep sight of the links between rape and masculine sexuality—why should men use *sex* as the weapon?

It is the fact that sex is used as the weapon which makes rape such a traumatic experience. Pellauer notes that women may 'experience rape as uniquely degrading precisely because its hurts and humiliations have been accomplished by sexual means – our capacities for expressing mutuality and love have been turned to an end that is the opposite of their purpose.'[9] It is experienced as a *total* violation of the person: 'Being forced sexually against one's will is the ultimate experience of powerlessness, short of death', says Fortune. The fact that occasionally women experience an orgasm during rape does not mean that it is primarily a sexual experience for them. Orgasm may be a physiological response to fear, or it may compound the injury because she feels betrayed even by her own body. The overriding experience remains one of fear and violation.[10]

Because rape is usually seen as primarily a *sexual* act, it is not treated with due seriousness. Women may joke or fantasize that they would like to be raped, as if it would show they were irresistibly attractive to men. But they are not talking about rape here, they are talking about being forced to do something they actually want to do and will enjoy. They are fantasizing having a sexual encounter without having responsibility for their own desires. But real rape situations are terrifying: 'The predominant feelings experienced by victims post-traumatically are those of powerlessness in the face of a life and death situation, vulnerability, devaluation, and fear of loss of ability to control the events in their lives.'[11]

Rape needs to be understood, yet dramatic portrayals or accounts of it almost inevitably make it appear entirely a sexual event. It is possible for the reality of rape to come through. In the mid-1980s, a TV documentary showed some American women confronting their rapists. The men were faced with the consequences of what they had done, although the effect on them was said to be short-lived. But the programme did convey the anger, pain, fear and distress the women had suffered. The shock was still present in their voices years after the event. The desire to convey the appalling trauma caused by rape lies behind Jill Saward's decision to write of her experience of being raped.[12] The knowledge of the awfulness of rape needs to be widespread, if it is to be treated seriously. There does seem to have been some progress in recent years, with the police striving to be more sympathetic, and public outcry over too-lenient sentencing policies, but there is still a long way to go.

Many people accept the myths that exist about sexual violence and abuse. Though she admits to using simplified examples, Kelly's table (pp. 98–9) is helpful in showing how these myths serve to minimize the offence and to remove responsibility from men for their actions. This is not to deny that childhood experiences or stress at work may be related to the behaviour of a particular individual. But such factors neither *excuse* the behaviour nor make it inevitable. After all, although women can also be violent towards men, children and elderly dependents, their frustrations characteristically do not take this form. And it can be said that women have more reason to feel frustrated and powerless than do men, given the economic and social situations many are in. Crucial here is the point that men's violence towards women is culturally sanctioned in a way that women's violence is not, particularly where men are seen as keeping 'their women' in line.

There has been some attempt to arrive at a definitive rapist profile. But since there are now over fifty subtypes, it appears that many different kinds of men can become rapists.[13] Rape may itself take different forms. Fortune summarizes these as 'power rape', 'anger rape' and 'sadistic rape' – though these are not always clear-cut. In power rape, the goal is sexual conquest, a desire to possess and dominate the victim. The rapist is seeking proof of his virility. He fantasizes that the victim gets aroused, and pretends that the victim enjoyed it. Anger rape is forceful and brutal, and includes a desire to harm and humiliate the victim. The rapist is seeking revenge on women. In sadistic rape, the rapist finds sexual gratification in tormenting and abusing, and may even kill the victim. This type is rarer than the other two.[14]

In none of these cases can the myth 'she asked for/deserved it' apply. Rapes are often planned carefully beforehand, they

Common Myths and Stereotypes about Sexual Violence[15]

Myth	Rape	Incest/sexual abuse	Domestic violence
1. They enjoy/ want it.	It wasn't rape, only 'rough sex'. Women say No when they mean Yes. Some women enjoy rape.	Girls get pleasure from it. They don't object, so they must like it. If it happens more than once they must want it.	Some women are masochistic, seeking out violent men. Women don't leave, so it can't be that bad.
2. They ask for/ deserve it.	Women provoke by the way they dress, by 'leading men on'. They take risks by going out alone, accepting lifts.	Girls are seductive or precocious.	Women provoke men by nagging, not fulfilling household 'duties', refusing sex.
3. It only happens to certain types of women/in certain kinds of families.	Women who live in poor areas; women who are sexually active; women who take risks; women who have previously been abused.	Girls who come from problem families; large families; isolated rural families; girls who are precocious; whose mothers were abused.	Working-class women; women who are 'bad' housewives; women who saw or experienced violence as children.
4. They tell lies/exaggerate.	Women make false reports for revenge, to protect their 'reputation'.[16]	Girls fantasize about incest, accuse men of sexual abuse to get attention.	It wasn't violence, only a fight. Women exaggerate to get a quick divorce.

5. If they had resisted they could have prevented it.	An unwilling woman cannot be raped. If there are no bruises she must have consented.	They should/ could have told someone.	If they had fought back it would stop the man, they are abused because they are weak and passive. They should have reported it.
6. The men who do it are sick, ill, under stress, out of control.	Abuse of alcohol/drugs, mental instability, childhood experiences cause men to act violently.		
	Hostility to women, psycho-sexual dysfunction.	Wife not sexually available. Deviant sexual arousal. Abused as a child.	Witnessed or experienced abuse as a child. Pressure of work/ unemployment.

are not the result of an oversexed man being aroused beyond control by a woman in a short skirt. Pellauer reports that 60 to 70 per cent are planned in advance, and victims can be infants or in their eighties. There is no guaranteed way for any woman to avoid being raped. A common element in rape is that offenders use obscene and insulting language; hatred and domination are the motive, not sexual desire.

In any case, even if men are sexually aroused, they do not therefore *have* to do something to the nearest woman, any more than do women in similar circumstances. A breastfeeding mother whose let-down reflex overtakes her in the super-market when she hears a strange baby cry does not force herself on the infant! The idea that men will harm themselves if an erection is not followed by ejaculation is a convenient myth, as is the belief that men are born with uncontrollable sexual urges. And as has been said, they always have the option of masturbation. According to Catholic tradition, masturbation was a worse sin than rape, because it was an 'unnatural sin', not capable of leading to pregnancy.

Presumably few would argue today that it was better to rape than to masturbate. This does raise the question, however, of whether a more sympathetic Christian attitude towards masturbation might have helped men to expect to deal with sexual tension in ways that are less destructive for women.

Men are perfectly capable of controlling their sexual feelings and behaviour. Men may say that when women say 'No' they mean 'Yes', and that really they enjoy being treated roughly. In a society where the sexes are brought up to feel they are different species, perhaps some men truly do think that women behave in a quite different way from men. But it is hard to believe that they cannot read women's reaction to assault. Moreover, that idea cannot explain the cruelty with which much rape is enacted.

Rape cannot be said to be an inevitable outcome of the male sexual nature, since it is not universal. Peggy Sanday found in a cross-cultural survey that rape was absent in 47 per cent of cultures, present in 36 per cent, whilst 17 per cent of cultures could be described as rape-prone. These tended to be cultures where men were encouraged to be tough and aggressive, did not relate to women, and where women took little part in public decision-making. They also tended to have a male supreme being,[17] and this should give Christians pause for thought. Do male images of God as all-powerful and all-controlling in any way reinforce men's desire for dominance over women? Christianity theoretically recognizes the will to dominance and aggression as sin, but seldom indicates that this is a sin to which males in our society may be particularly prone.

Though the chances of a woman or girl being assaulted by a stranger or acquaintance are comparatively small, the fear of it happening haunts women and significantly affects their behaviour. So many of women's interactions with men are coloured by suspicion. Unless we know them very well, and sometimes even then, we are careful what we do and say, just in case. There are enough cases of women or children being assaulted or murdered to give credence to our fears. Such cases receive great publicity, and the emphasis is on what women can do to be safe. We hear little about the many women who live, walk and work alone without anything terrible happening to them, and stories of attacks on women are not set in perspective. When estate agent Suzy Lamplugh disappeared while showing a client a house, a trust was set up to help women at work to protect themselves. Yet men are more likely to be at risk of death or major injury than women, because they traditionally do the more dangerous jobs, such as construction work.

When Marie Wilkes, seven months pregnant, was murdered after breaking down on a motorway, special advice was given out to women motorists. Over five thousand people can die on our roads each year, and women continue to drive. Yet this one murder makes them afraid, perhaps give up driving alone. After this tragedy, women motorists who broke down on the motorway were advised to stay locked in their cars. Interestingly, police later reversed this advice, because the risk of being injured or killed through staying in a car on the hard shoulder was much greater than the risk of being attacked outside the car. Yet it is difficult for women in that situation to look at it logically; fear of being attacked is so powerfully embedded in their psyche. I feel myself that as a cyclist in Oxford, I am more likely to be involved in a traffic accident than assaulted. But my heart always beats faster on lonely roads than in the busy city centre.

It is understandable that women should want to do all they can to safeguard themselves, but it represents a giving in to male violence which may not be helpful in the longer term. It is, moreover, accepting the idea that female victims are in some way responsible for what happened to them in a way that is not suggested for male victims. Statistically, it is young men who are most likely to be victims of violence, yet as far as I know, they are not publicly urged to stay at home, go to special youths' self-defence classes, or carry alarms. One difficulty is that if a woman gives no thought to the risk of assault, and something happens, she is held responsible. As one judge infamously put it, she is guilty of 'contributory negligence'. Yet women who do take precautions may be considered neurotic, sexually repressed creatures whose expectation of assault denotes wishful thinking.

The fact is that women's safety cannot be guaranteed whatever they do. If being alone is risky, so is being with a man, since most crimes of violence and sexual abuse against women are committed by men they know. Living with other women is no solution, since men may be even more aggressive where they feel excluded.[18] It is significant that women are not advised to avoid marriage or relationships with men because of the risk of violence, but they are urged to give up their independence for this reason. It is highly unlikely that an individual woman will be attacked by a fearsome sex-monster. It makes sense for women to alter their behaviour where there is a proven risk, but there is no need to let irrational fear restrict their lives.

A similar attitude may need to operate with regard to what parents let their children do. I talk to my daughter a lot about the fact that there are nasty people in the world who might try to hurt her, and what she should do in particular situations. Yet she is an outgoing child, who quickly strikes up friendships with strangers in the park, the street and the swimming pool, when we are there together. I am caught as to how I should react. To say '*never* talk to strangers' is to close her world down, to make it a menacing place – never *go* with strangers seems more appropriate. Yet would she be safer in a closed world, suspicious and careful when others are friendly to her?

The Christian response to the threat of male violence against women tends to be to admit defeat, to counsel women to put themselves under male protection or to lock themselves in their homes (both of which are risky in any case). The women who will not go out alone at night, or steer clear of walking in the countryside by themselves, are buying into a perspective which sees the world as dangerous and full of evil men. This is a view which the media encourages, as the Posy Simmonds cartoon in Chapter 12 notes and I frequently fall prey to it myself. But I wonder whether seeing all men as potential attackers parallels the way that men have seen all women as potential sexual temptresses. The person gets obscured by having all sorts of powerful projections placed on them. Is God's message here the same one addressed to Jews about Gentiles, and interpreted today for men about women: 'What God has cleansed you must not call common'? (Acts 10.15).

There is a parallel here with the Christian view which sees the world as dangerous and full of temptation. But our faith teaches us that this is *God's* world, created with love for our enjoyment, dignified by God's presence in human form in Jesus Christ. Though a fallen world, God is still to be found everywhere within it. Christ comes to us in our fellow human beings, the Spirit of God is at work in human hearts and systems. If these are reasons why Christians cannot withdraw from the world, they are surely also reasons why women cannot reject the world as the province of evil men. Women can begin to lay claim to their right to walk alone, to enjoy God's creation, to relate to men as potential friends not potential rapists. They need to get their fears in perspective, and not allow their lives to be so restricted by fear of men. Equally, men need to look at what role they play in reinforcing women's fears. This will mean examining points where their behaviour comes across as threatening to women, and ceasing to be overprotective.

Recently, a male relative gave me an alarm to carry in my handbag, and I found I had very ambivalent feelings about it. Is it a sensible device, equivalent to having a smoke detector, or was it given me out of a perception that I am in danger all the time simply because I am a woman, a perception I recognize, but want to reject? Just as with any accident or illness, there is always the chance that it will happen to me, and some precautions may be necessary. I am certainly not suggesting that Christians receive special protection from harm, or that they are less affected when tragedy does strike. But it is wrong to let our lives be ruled by fear of what might happen, and to fail to live fully in God's world because we are so anxious about the future. That is true generally, and it is especially true for women.

Chapter 10

Home is where the hurt is

Each time your husband hits you just think of it as an opportunity to be a little closer to Jesus and the angels.[1]

A husband is bound to chastise his wife moderately, unless he be a cleric, in which case he may chastise her harder.[2]

I believe that all men are sadistic. The only reason why some men are not overtly abusive or physically violent is that they are living with partners who are tamed, so they don't need to be controlled.[3]

Home and family are given special significance in much Christian writing. 'The family' is something to be respected and preserved as a defence against the decaying morals of the rest of society. The feminist critique, on the other hand, has labelled family life as oppressive. The home is the place where women and children are most likely to suffer abuse. Perhaps that critique has been unduly scathing, for home and family are important to many people, and great strength and value can be found there. But we must recognize that homes can also be oppressive.

Family life is often far from harmonious. Many people live in a negative atmosphere of mutual distrust and emotional distancing. The Christian ideal for a married couple is often based on specific masculine and feminine roles. But where differences between the sexes are emphasized, the communication gap between them grows. In addition, where men are given a dominant role in marriage, with both women and children expected to obey in all things, the way may be opened up for abuse. Bussert goes so far as to say, 'If submission continues to be the "theory", then battering will inevitably continue to be the "practice".'[4] Christians may point out that husbands are supposed to love their wives as their own selves, but men are not always good at understanding their own needs. Indeed, if men were better at cherishing themselves, they might be less inclined to vent their frustration on women.

Women are warned not to venture out on the streets for fear of rape and assault. But they are far more likely to be raped or beaten in their own homes, often by their own husbands. Children are taught that home is where they are secure and loved, they will be safe if they can 'say no to strangers'. Yet abuse within the family is far more common. These things happen on such a large scale that they cannot simply be ignored as exceptions. There is considerable reluctance to admit the extent of domestic abuse, for if it is common, then it suggests that both offenders and victims are ordinary people like us, and that is a threatening thought. Thus when 165 children were diagnosed as having been sexually abused in Cleveland, in North-East England, in 1987, the immediate reaction of many people was to denounce the paediatricians and social workers who made the diagnosis and to deny that abuse was happening.

The plight of battered women has been discussed openly for many years now, and though still inadequate, there is some provision made for women in this situation through refuges and more sympathetic police attitudes to domestic violence. It is also acknowledged more widely that women are raped, sometimes with extreme violence, by their husbands. In Scotland, this is a criminal offence, and a review of the law was being considered for England in 1990. Prior to this, marriage was thought to give the man sexual rights over the woman, regardless of whether she consented on each occasion. On a TV programme in 1989, the 'World in Action' team looked at this subject. A judge was interviewed who stated that rape in marriage was not serious, because it was quite a different experience being raped by a stranger, and being raped by someone with whom you often did consent to have intercourse. But women who had had this experience felt it was actually worse, for they had to live with the man who had done this to them. The judge, confronted by this, simply replied that he did not accept it. Fortunately the government was prepared to look at the evidence for the seriousness of this offence.

Rape is not rough sex, but is experienced as a fundamental violation of bodily integrity and fear for one's life. Women who are raped at home are traumatized because they lose the ability to trust: 'Marital rape touches a woman's basic confidence in forming relationships and trusting intimates. It can leave a woman feeling much more powerless and isolated than if she were raped by a stranger.'[5]

Domestic violence happens at a number of levels. Women may accept a certain amount of physical aggression from men, and may even reciprocate. But the behaviour at issue here is much more serious, consisting of assaults which would be criminal offences if committed outside the home. These include broken bones, disfiguring injuries, and the use of weapons such as knives. It is likely to be repeated behaviour. Yet the assumption that it is all right for a husband to use violence against his wife is long-standing. The *degree* of chastisement was at one time limited by law, but it was an old adage that 'a woman, a dog and a walnut tree/the more you beat them the better they be.' Moreover, the home is considered to be the Englishman's private castle, and police have been reluctant to intervene in domestic disputes.[6]

Although women can use serious physical violence against men or dependents, by far the largest number of domestic violence cases are of men assaulting women or children. For example, Dobash and Dobash found that 97 per cent of assaulters in the home were male, whilst 94 per cent of the victims were female; 75 per cent of victims were wives, 10 per cent children, and only one per cent of victims were husbands. The majority of elderly abused are female, but even though the majority of carers are female, abusers are slightly more likely to be male.[7]

Yet rather than attention being focused on why men are violent, it tends to be the victim who is held responsible. This parallels what happens with rape and child abuse, as the table on pp. 98–9 showed. Very often, women are blamed for staying with a violent partner. Yet the reasons for this are many and complex. They stay through fear that the man will come after them if they leave, and be even more violent. They stay through guilt, feeling that they really do deserve this treatment. They may feel the social stigma of people finding out what has been going on. Women may be sorry for their husbands, wondering how their men would manage without them. And in between violent episodes, a husband may be pleasant and caring, and promise it will not happen again. And overriding all these factors is the basic question of where and how a woman is to live, especially if she has children. What on one level may seem foolish acquiescence, may in fact be the best way of coping in a situation with few options. Moreover, battered women tend to suffer from stress and poor health, and thus may feel even more powerless and lacking in energy to make changes or leave. There are many reasons why women stay, but the question to be addressed is why *he* is violent, rather than why *she* stays.

Battered women may be thought to have caused the violence by provocation. It is often suggested that if only the woman could alter her behaviour, she would be safe. But it is clear that it is the man who controls whether abuse will happen, and the woman can do little about it. If she is very self-effacing, she may postpone the eruption of violence, but she will not stop it. Jim Wilson, who runs a group for batterers in Bolton, tells them, 'Domestic violence comes from two things: the *authority* you believe you should have over your wife, and the *services* you expect to get from her.'[8] Thus violence will ensue at any point where the man feels insecure about controlling his wife, or she fails to live up to all his expectations. Since women are autonomous creatures, not owned by men, and ordinary, fallible human beings, this scenario frequently occurs. The issue is not women's behaviour, but why men feel they have a right to respond to that behaviour with anger and violence.

It is a myth that men who batter are simply short-tempered. The violence is generally deliberate, and controlled both as to what kind of injuries are inflicted and where on the person, and as to when he stops. Most batterers are not violent in other situations. Indeed, in the public sphere, people often have to control themselves even in the face of extreme provocation. Of course violence does occur – between teacher and pupil, social worker and client, for example – but generally we express our anger in other ways. It may indeed be true that batterers have stressful and frustrating jobs, or have grown up in violent homes. But so have many other people who do *not* go on to abuse their partners.

It has been suggested that the patriarchal capitalist system demands that men repress their feelings of alienation at work, so that 'the frustration and anger that men should direct toward organizational action at the work place' finds an outlet 'in the privacy of the home through petty tyranny and verbal abuse, neglect and promiscuity, wife beating and child mistreatment'.[9] Men may feel they can expect their homes to be havens, and when this does not happen, they blame women for the failure. There is some truth in this, but it does not explain why some men use physical violence and others do not. Many people are under stress at work, and this does have negative effects on their families, but most are not violent towards partners and children.

Violence arises out of men's need to feel in control, and is thus inextricably bound up with society's understanding of masculinity. Adam Jukes' assessment is that 'we live in a culture where women are defined as what we men need to complete ourselves. Because they withhold that, we find them utterly uncontrollable. And we try to control them by inflicting pain.' This is confirmed by research which points out that although other factors may contribute to a man's violence, 'the key factor is the degree to which he has bought into the definition of what it means to be a man in this culture and chooses to enforce it violently in the home.'[10]

It is not that men who batter simply cannot express their feelings, but that they typically express their emotions through anger. They are highly emotionally dependent on their wives, and the desire to control tends to be linked with extreme possessiveness and jealousy. Such men may say that they love their wives, and others may accept that this is why they are 'provoked' into violence by their wives' behaviour. But again, it is no excuse for men's violent behaviour.

Christian writers in this country have made little attempt to tackle the issue of male aggression and violence towards women. *Faith in the City* does raise the issue of 'battered wives', and further acknowledges the relation of this to Christian thinking on male dominance and female subservience.[11] But it is not a main issue in the report. Writings specifically for Christian men often stress the importance of male dominance, however kindly the spirit with which it is exercised. And writings for Christian women emphasize the importance of submission. Obviously, such writers do not envisage violence as in any way part of God's purpose for marriage; yet teachings about submission are picked up by women who are in violent situations.

All of us have within us the capacity for violence. Our society's emphasis on the formation of couples and nuclear families means we have intense relationships which can create their own tensions. An imbalance of power makes it possible for one person to unload their frustrations on to those below them in the hierarchy, with adult males having the widest number of possible victims. Few parents have not taken out their own frustrations on a child in the physical violence of an over-hard smack, and we tend to accept this as normal. 'It never hurt me when my parents smacked me,' we say, 'and it doesn't hurt my kids now.' This is a difficult area. I can remember vividly the childhood feelings of humiliation and anger that came with being slapped. But when I lose my temper and smack or shout at my children, I try to convince myself (and them) that they quickly forget.

Some Christians have written books justifying smacking or other physical punishment as essential for rearing godly children. 'Daring to discipline' is seen as Christian parenting.[12] At the other end of the spectrum, parents are urged to respect children's rights and discuss everything with them. Yet this may put too much responsibility on to children who do not yet have enough experience of the world to make such decisions. Finding a right balance here is important, for we need a model of behaviour in the home which prevents abuse. It is for parents to recognize that their children are unique human individuals, for adults to recognize this of their partners. We must never think that we have a legitimate right to abuse or take advantage of our power over another.

The recognition that children have rights, and do not belong to their parents to use or abuse as they will, lies behind public condemnation of child abuse. Though historically always present, it was in the 1980s that child abuse came to public prominence in Britain. The events in Cleveland gave it major coverage, although the scale of the problem was apparent to professionals who worked with children and adult survivors long before that. The subject is an extremely emotive one because it raises issues about masculine sexuality, and exposes divisions between the sexes within the heart of the family.

Beatrix Campbell draws out the latter point very well in her study of the Cleveland crisis, pointing out that the unsayable thing during the Butler-Sloss inquiry was that 'Perpetrators are typically male and abuse is an expression of a patriarchal sexual culture.'[13] That statement is true as regards all the information we have at present. The vast majority of abusers identified have been men. However, at the time of writing, more information is emerging about the involvement of women in child sexual abuse.[14] It may well be that their numbers are much higher than was previously thought, but I would be surprised if women were shown to form a large percentage of sexual abusers. This is not because I consider women more naturally virtuous than men, or incapable of abusing children. We know a great deal about the harm mothers cause their children emotionally and physically.[15] We know that women share the complex psychological and sexual motivations which lead men to sexual abuse; and given that abusers often have a history of being abused themselves, we might expect more women to be involved. Nonetheless, women's sexuality does not characteristically express itself through domination, aggression, and violence towards others. I would expect to find more men sexually abusing children in the home for the same reason that it is predominantly men who rape and assault and sexually harass women and children in the public sphere: that is the construction of male sexuality which our society accepts. It is a human failing to use and abuse others for selfish reasons. But there is a gender difference in the way in which we do this.

Another area which needs to be mentioned is that of child sex rings and ritual child abuse. These too are issues which have been emerging at the time of writing. There have been a number of prosecutions of organized paedophile sex rings, which typically involve men abusing boys. There have also been horrific stories circulating about bizarre rituals and child sacrifice. Extensive media coverage followed allegations of ritual child abuse in Rochdale, Lancashire, in 1990, and although there is little corroborated evidence of satanic child abuse at present, it is becoming clear that this dimension is present in some cases of abuse. Women may be involved in the abuse, although the leaders generally appear to be men.

Because of the religious implications of satanism, some Christians have been more ready to take action against child abuse in that context than to look at its more common manifestations. But we must remember that child abuse is evil wherever it occurs, and that survivors of abuse of every kind need careful counselling and help and may or may not desire spiritual counselling. Organized and ritual abuse may create additional problems, for example children may be more easily frightened into silence, and suffer more pronounced psychological disturbance. But it cannot be considered in isolation from the widespread abuse of children in our society generally.

The general media coverage of events in Cleveland showed a lack of understanding about features of child abuse cases well known to those with experience in the field: that abusers can be very convincing liars, that children rarely lie about the fact that abuse has occurred, but that they do frequently retract. The situation was portrayed as a battle between innocent fathers and man-hating feminists, with the needs of children who had been abused put on one side. Mothers of children suspected of being sexually abused got little public sympathy either.[17] It is interesting, though sad, that the major way in which men reacted was not with horror that fathers could abuse children, but with feeling threatened that *they* might be suspected.

A number of men talked to me about how they felt they could not play with or cuddle their children any more. It seems incredible that men should not know the difference between normal affectionate behaviour and abuse. Yet for many men, affectionate behaviour is identical with sex. Hite concludes that 'many men feel that the only appropriate way for a man to ask for love and affection is by initiating sex and intercourse . . . men look forward to sex and intercourse as providing an appropriate time and place to be emotional.' Hite also makes the suggestion that the 'fact that this is almost men's only time to be emotional and "let their hair down" may account in some measure for men's feeling that they rarely get enough sex and intercourse.' At the same time, most men could not envisage being friendly with a woman with whom they did not have sex, and felt that a friendship with a woman would inevitably lead this way.[18] It is possible that the fact that men have no model for relating affectionately without sex is one element in abuse.

Here too blame is attached to the victims (see pp. 98–9). Mothers are also blamed, since it is thought that they must know what is going on. Perhaps some mothers do collude with the abuse, but most mothers take action as soon as they find out, and most reports of abuse are made by mothers. It is quite possible for mothers not to know, for the child is likely to have been pressured into secrecy. Partners often do manage to deceive each other for some time about affairs, and men can usually find opportunities when their wives are not around to abuse children. It is often forgotten that the abusers are active controllers of the situation, not passive victims of circumstance. They know what they are doing, and make sure that the abuse is concealed. Moreover, it will usually take incontrovertible evidence before a woman will suspect her own partner of such awful behaviour.

As with other offences of this sort, there is no single factor which causes some men to abuse children. It is often pointed out that abusers may well have been themselves victims of abuse, and this is used to explain their behaviour. However, although many abusers were abused as children, and sexual abuse can run in generations, this 'cycle' is not inevitable. The majority of the victims of abuse are female, yet most abusers are men. The idea of a cycle of abuse can be harmful, for abused children may be *expected* to become abusers. I heard of one case where a baby had been born as the result of incest, and the adoptive mother found herself wondering whether she was now rearing a likely abuser.

Christian approaches to child sex abuse in this country have been rather limited to date. There is pastoral concern, but the deeper issues of gender and power have not been adequately explored. There is a tendency to simplify the issue, without recognizing the deep trauma the experience is likely to have engendered. This can lead to insistence on the need for the victim to forgive the abuser, without taking fully into account the painful long-drawn-out nature of the process. Child abuse is often seen as an individual problem for the man who cannot control himself properly.

Some books take up the point that victims of abuse may find it difficult to call God Father. Yet the response is to say that the masculinity of God is very important, and children and adults must come to terms with their problems with the opposite sex: 'It's important to your healing to come to trust this masculine God, to honor him, to submit to him.'[19] It is true that the image of God as Mother may not be a help to incest survivors who may feel anger at mothers for failing to protect them. But there are important theological issues here which need taking up. For example, how far is the Fatherhood of God presented in terms which encourage dependency and obedience – which is not a good model for human family relationships? By contrast to the British situation, theologians in the United States and elsewhere have done detailed work on abuse and sexual violence. Their writing is based on proper research of the issues, and offers some important guidelines for us, as the next chapter shows.

· *Chapter 11* ·

Whose fault?

People need to recognize that those of us who have been so much influenced by violence in the media, in particular pornographic violence, are not some kind of inherent monsters. We are your sons and we are your husbands and we grew up in regular families.[1]

The cross is not only a sign of God's suffering with us in Christ, it is the hope of resurrection for all who have been hurt and victimized by the evil that haunts our world.[2]

The Christian Church likes to build on its reputation for caring for victims. It may be criticized for failing to address the causes of poverty or famine, but it is traditionally good at providing relief and binding up people's wounds. For many Christians, as for many others who care for those in need, the guilt or innocence of the one cared for is irrelevant. Someone dying with AIDS is seen to need pastoral and medical care regardless of whether they became infected in their mother's womb, from a blood transfusion, through drug abuse, or through sexual activity. But in the Church, as in society generally, there is also often a strong tendency to moralize about victims. Those who have brought illness or misfortune on themselves are deemed less worthy of support than those who are completely innocent. At one level this is understandable. The terrorist who loses a limb whilst planting a bomb cannot expect the same level of sympathy as the child maimed in the same explosion. Yet it is both dangerous and fundamentally anti-Christian to let our assumptions about guilt and innocence determine how we treat others. For we tend to set ourselves up as innocent, and fail to take seriously the humanity of those whom we label guilty.

The question of guilt and innocence is particularly relevant to the way that women are treated. For there is a readiness to see them as guilty, especially where they are victims of any kind of sexual abuse. Rather than a reaction of overwhelming sympathy, the victim of rape or sexual violence is likely to be faced with suspicion: did she bring it on herself, or is she telling lies to get men into trouble? That this should be the *first* reaction to a woman in distress indicates how destructive are the negative attitudes towards women perpetuated in our society. It is only some women who are seen as truly innocent victims. Both elderly women and obviously pregnant women are deemed non-sexual, and therefore cannot have 'caused' sexual assault. Young babies are also innocent, but even small girls have been accused of being flirtatious, and therefore of luring men into abusing them. In reaction against this, some have wanted to stress that women who are assaulted are always innocent. But whilst it is true that no woman or girl deserves to undergo such terrible trauma, sympathy and justice should not depend on the moral integrity of the victim.

The problem is that sexual crimes against women are treated quite differently to other crimes, and both perceptions of women's inherent sexuality, and suspicion of their intentions towards men, prejudice attitudes towards them. I have friends who keep some valuable antiques in a glass-fronted cabinet in full view of anyone who comes to their front door. Though the house is locked when they are out, it would be easy to gain an entrance. If they are burgled, are they guilty of contributory negligence? They know that there are greedy people around, and yet they display their property. Are they not tempting weak people to steal? In the past, they have both sold and given away some of their antiques – does this mean it matters less if they are burgled? As far as I know, such arguments are not employed to defend burglars. Though my friends might be thought foolish, no one would suggest that it was their fault.[3] Instead, anger would be directed at whoever committed the offence. It would theoretically be possible that they had arranged the theft to cheat their insurance company, but that would not be the first thought in people's minds, and would be investigated only if other circumstances were suspicious.

If assaults on women were treated in the same way, it would be the offender on whom attention was focused, rather than the victim. It would be true in some cases that the victim's behaviour affected what happened to them, but this is true of most of the things that happen to us. After bad things happen, we can see this, and find ourselves wishing 'if only . . .' Our decisions and actions can contribute to events without our being morally culpable. It is recognized now that it may be more helpful to speak of survivors rather than victims, for this affirms that however powerless the victim may have felt, they have come through the ordeal. Though some resistance strategies work, it is very difficult to tell whilst in a situation what the best course is. Women may submit to a violent assault because they are frozen with terror, or they may choose this as the only way of coming out alive. It is not for those who look on from the outside to dictate how a rape survivor should have behaved, any more than they would dream of telling the survivor of a plane crash that they would have suffered less injury if they'd jumped more sensibly. Yet because assaults on women are approached from a negative viewpoint, failure to resist actively is taken as compliance, whilst resistance is seen as foolish (and may bring worse injury).

It can be very difficult to cope with the fact both that our behaviour affects what happens to us, and that we are not always to blame for consequences. We make the decisions which seem best at the time, and cannot ever know all the possible outcomes. And even for those who have knowingly taken risks, or acted badly, it can only very rarely be argued that they deserve a penalty of extreme violence or death. If someone is injured or killed as they try to injure or kill others, many people would say that it served them right. That may not be a proper Christian view, but it is held by many. But the vast majority of women who are assaulted, battered, raped or killed have not been threatening men's lives. Their 'offences' are at worst nagging, walking alone, saying no, wearing high heels, and at times they are guilty of no more than being there when a man feels violent. They do not deserve what happens to them. In most cases, the bad things that happen to us are out of all proportion to our behaviour – and this is what makes the problem of suffering so intense for the Christian.

It is more difficult for those who believe that faith or good behaviour give protection against suffering. A common reaction amongst those who are abused or assaulted is a feeling of worthlessness: they must be evil for such a thing to happen to them. Alternatively, such an experience may turn them against the God who failed to protect them. It is important for Christians to avoid suggesting that Christians lead charmed lives; yet that view underlies much of our prayer. Pleas for personal safety must be the most common forms of prayer, yet disaster strikes with no discrimination between Christian and non-Christian, good and bad. We respond either by feeling it is our fault for having too little faith, or we turn against God, or we say that God must be trying to teach us something through this. Now it is quite true that those who pass through terrible experiences often learn from them; but that is not the same as saying that God sends suffering for that purpose. The violation of rape, prolonged abuse by a parent, or frequent assaults by a husband must never be glorified as events sent from the hand of God. We may also need to be careful how we speak about the suffering and death of Christ, lest we uphold 'actions and attitudes that accept, glorify, and even encourage suffering'.[4]

Many Christians seem still to be stuck in the early part of the Jewish tradition, when suffering was taken as a sign of the victim's own guilt. But the later Jewish scriptures, and the New Testament, are clear that suffering comes to good and bad alike. The parable of the Good Samaritan bids us treat even those we mistrust and dislike as our neighbours. The victim had been foolish – going alone along a road notorious for robbers. Yet it is significant that neither he nor the robbers are blamed, rather it is those who fail to help. Daily, we hear stories of women who go alone along roads, and are assaulted. And those who pass by on the other side are those who say 'she deserved it', 'she asked for it'. If we are truly to take to heart our Christian calling, we should be standing with the victim, binding up her wounds, and trying to ensure that her suffering is not repeated.

From the pastoral point of view, Christians need to avoid expecting instant healing from such hurts. It may take many years for such experiences to be worked through, and some suffering may be so traumatic that nothing ever heals it completely. As Dorothee Soelle says, we may be able to change the social conditions under which people experience suffering:

> We can change ourselves and learn in suffering instead of becoming worse. We can gradually beat back and abolish the suffering that still today is produced for the profit of a few. But on all these paths we come up against boundaries that cannot be crossed. Death is not the only such barrier. There are also brutalization and insensibility, mutilation and injury that can no longer be reversed. The only way these boundaries can be crossed is by sharing the pain of the sufferers with them, not leaving them alone and making their cry louder.[5]

There is a useful discussion of some of these points in Harold Kushner's book *When Bad Things Happen to Good People.* For Kushner, there are two reasons why we are so ready to feel or attribute guilt when bad things happen to us or other people. The first is our strenuous need to believe that the world makes sense, that there is a cause for every effect and a reason for everything that happens. We feel insecure and anxious in a world of random chaos. The second element is the notion that *we* are the cause of what happens, that every disaster is somehow our fault.[6] An extreme example of this came in a recent television programme where a woman who had run over and killed a child, through no fault of her own, described how she had been racked by guilt for fifteen years. She was unable to forgive herself, and whenever anything bad happened in her life, she saw this as God punishing her for taking a life.

The theme of Kushner's book is that the question, 'Why did this happen to me, what did I do to deserve this?' is unanswerable and pointless. The better question is, 'Now that this has happened to me, what am I going to do about it?' God is not blamed, but turned to for strength and comfort. Kushner suggests that the right response to those who have been hurt by life is to insist: 'This was not your fault. You are a good, decent person who deserves better.'[7] We should allow ourselves to be angry at the injustice and suffering in the world.

It is important to stress that victims are not to blame, and yet a picture of victims as passive playthings of fate may leave them feeling even more powerless. This point is explored by Mary Potter Engel. She says we must differentiate between evil and sin when dealing with abuse. Evil is found in the structures of oppression which are larger than individuals, distort our perceptions, and make it hard for us to do good. Sin is found in our individual acts which create or reinforce the structures of oppression. It is not, she says, that victim and perpetrator are equally to blame. Victims have not committed the sin of abusing others, but they have been affected by the systems of evil, which may have lured them into complying with their victimization. Perpetrators need to be held accountable for sinful actions. Speaking of evil structures to them is not helpful, for it allows them to escape their responsibility for what they have done. Yet though the main emphasis for victim and perpetrator is different, Engel suggests that the counterside is not forgotten, 'for it is as freeing to men to learn that they are tempted by evil structures as it is for women to learn that they are responsible in part for the direction of their lives.'[8]

Engel's point that perpetrator and victim have a different relationship to abuse is important. She, like a number of other feminists, is critical of forms of family therapy which hold victim and perpetrator equally to blame. It may well be that the internal dynamics of a family cast light on the abusive behaviour of one of its members. But individual responsibility also matters, and it is important not to suggest that the victim's behaviour deserved this treatment. It may also need to be recognized, in some cases, that the well-being of the individuals in a family is of more importance than the preservation of the family structure. It is not always right to insist that families stay together, though the effects of family break-up need careful consideration.

The preoccupation with women's sexuality within the Church has made it difficult for the Church to respond to sexual abuse and violence towards women. Within the Bible itself, there are a number of stories of violence against women. But as Fortune points out, the main concern is not with the victim. Indeed, one prominent story, that of Potiphar's wife, (Gen. 39) reinforces the myth that accusations of rape are likely to be made in order to gain revenge. The rape and murder of two women in the story of Sodom is regarded merely as incidental. More recently, the 1962 Catholic Dictionary of Moral Theology even suggests that reparation can be made if a woman marries her rapist. Incest is seen as wrong because of the possible hereditary defect in any resulting children, not because incest is destructive in itself. But the criterion should be whether damage is done to the victim, rather than whether some abstract moral principle is broken. Sexual violence is sinful not because of its *sexual* nature, but 'because it is an exploitative and abusive violation of the victim's bodily integrity.' It is blasphemous because it denies the sacredness of the other person. It is *not* loving your neighbour. Our response to this kind of sin should include righteous anger, advocacy for the victim, and holding the offender legally and spiritually accountable.[9]

The question of how to deal with offenders is a difficult one. Offences against women have not always been taken seriously in the past, and paying attention to the motivations and needs of offenders may seem to fall into the same trap. But it is only if men are seen as human beings, and not as perverted sex monsters, that there is any hope of change. It is of primary importance to insist that men do not have to be aggressive and violent towards women (or each other). Men are not irredeemable! This means both that male offenders must be held accountable for their offences, and that rehabilitation, not revenge, is the ultimate aim. Caricatures of attitudes to crime and punishment suggest that one side wants to 'hang the lot of them', and the other to explain it all away. Yet compassion has room both for appropriate punishment, and for understanding why the offence came to be committed. The challenge is to find ways of speaking which do justice to both.

Men who abuse or assault women or children are ordinary people, as the murderer quoted at the start of this chapter pointed out. After conviction, such men are labelled monsters, they are segregated in prison for their own safety. Yet whilst they are committing offences, they appear normal. The initial reaction of families and friends is generally disbelief and shock. Clearly those who commit such offences are damaged human beings, in whom something has gone more than ordinarily wrong. Yet all of us are damaged to some degree; that is the human condition. We are right to be outraged at serious offences, yet that must not mean locating all the evil in one individual and failing to see the responsibility of the human community in which such things happen. The questions we must ask, says Pellauer, are:

> How could this sort of act happen at all among people who are caring for each other? Why are we so seldom aware of these acts or the painful consequences of them? Why do we raise and allow to come to maturity assailants who are able and willing to so damage another human person?[10]

Sexual violence is a sin against the community because of the fear, mistrust and limitations it imposes. It creates a hostile environment in which right relationships cannot flourish, particularly between men and women. Men are anxious lest their behaviour be misinterpreted, women feel they need to be on their guard even with men they know quite well. Sexual violence is also a sin against God, for sexuality was given by God to build up relationships, but here it destroys them. Says Fortune: 'When a person is so alienated from God and his neighbour that he chooses to strike out, seeking violent conquest rather than loving union with another, he is manifesting the brokenness of humankind.'[11]

However much we acknowledge that other forces are at work when sexual violence takes place, it is essential that offenders take responsibility for their actions. Though we are all influenced to a lesser or greater degree by our circumstances, we do have a choice about what we do or do not do, and this is an important point for Christians to stress: 'Various factors, such as alcoholism, poverty, sexism, a heritage of pain, mistrust, and the experience of abuse contribute to and motivate a person to hurt others, but they do not *force* the person to commit abusive acts.'[12] Offenders are morally responsible, and need to receive appropriate punishment. One problem is that sentences handed out to men who assault women fail to give a clear message that sexual violence against women is wrong. In one case, two men who raped a young woman during a burglary were given three and five year sentences, whilst the ringleader, who tried to dissuade them from the rape, received ten years. The judge said the rape sentences were not longer because the rape victim's trauma was 'not so great'.[13]

Though I am not an advocate of longer prison sentences in general, they are more appropriate in cases of unprovoked violence and sexual assault. There is a need to protect the community from those who are dangerous and violent, and it may have a deterrent effect. The police and the judicial system have been reluctant in the past to 'interfere' in cases of domestic violence. Though there are problems in investigating such cases, this attitude nevertheless gives tacit approval to marital violence. But it was found in Canada that the threat of a prison sentence for violent husbands was an effective deterrent, and the number of incidents fell. Prison sentences are also ways in which the community can punish those who step outside its laws. Punishment, deterrence and protection are all questions which need to be considered when dealing with offenders. But whatever sentence is passed, it is essential that offenders are not then forgotten about.

Rowan Williams, in a lecture given inside a prison to an audience including many serious offenders, spelt out the necessity for Christians to treat prisoners as responsible individuals: 'For the Christian, there is no option of ignoring *anyone's* capacity to give and receive as a member of a community, to be part of a social enterprise, a shared work. That's what is, non-negotiably, involved in being "in the image of God".' We need to ask how prisoners can be enabled to assimilate the past, to recognize what has been done, and to imagine it particularly from the victim's viewpoint. This is what is meant by penitence.[14] One of the key insights which Christian tradition can offer is that it is possible to move forward. Both victim and offender are invited to a new life, in which they can be freed from what has happened to them or what they have done in the past.

It is essential that more thought be given to the practicalities of how offenders are treated. The prison riots of early 1990 were an uncomfortable reminder for many people of the fact that offenders still exist after sentencing, they cannot be locked away with sighs of relief. But crime committed by men against women is only part of the picture. As this book has shown, there is a whole range of behaviour and attitudes which reinforces negative treatment of women, and this can and must be challenged.

· *Chapter 12* ·

Restoring the Image

Spirit of our God descending,
Fill our hearts with heavenly joy.
Love with every passion blending,
Pleasure that can never cloy . . .

Our sensuality is grounded in Nature, in Compassion, and in
Grace. In our sensuality, God is. God is the means whereby our
Substance and our Sensuality are kept together so as never to be
apart.[1]

It is very difficult for both sexes to come to terms with men's
denigration and oppression of women. It has been easiest for
most of us to pretend it doesn't happen. Pornography or
sexual violence may intrude on our consciousness from time
to time, women get used to dealing with occasional unwelcome
attentions from men, and we snipe at each other in our
intimate relationships. But we do not connect these things
together. Most of us lack any sense of the system of patriarchy,
which makes women and men view each other with suspicion,
and leads to men trying to exert power over women. Perhaps
we sense, rightly, that to admit the existence of patriarchy will
threaten the delicate balance of our lives together. I spend
much of my working and leisure hours in the company of
men, barely conscious of gender differences between us. But
sometimes a comment on the subject of discussion suddenly
puts us on opposite sides, and we experience a fall into
division and enmity.

The feminist critique threatens to bring this sense of division
into our intimate relationships. Posy Simmonds illustrates
how this might feel in her cartoon 'Always in the News'.
Women who have established reasonably comfortable patterns

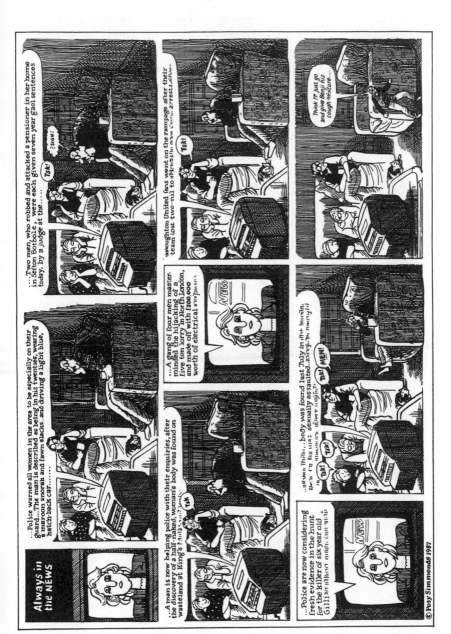

125

for living with men do not want their lives disturbed. Many feminists, who are aware of the evil of patriarchy, insist that *their* men are different; how could they admit otherwise and still stay in the relationship? Radical feminists have little sympathy for this fraternizing with the enemy, and may regard heterosexual relationships as an impossibility. So is there any way of being honest about the evils of male domination whilst maintaining good relationships between men and women?

Part of the answer lies in focusing on the common humanity which we share. This means insisting that men are not evil by nature, any more than women are. Men's suspicions and fear of women, as well as their dependence on and admiration for women, parallel women's attitudes towards men. But the crucial difference is that men have power in society, and their experience is writ large and taken as definitive for all. Men have dominated for so long in the key institutions of society that it seems normal; we believe in their ability to be impartial. Yet it is inevitable that any group in power will tend to perpetuate its own interests, and this has happened both overtly and unconsciously in the decisions men make.

Inaccurate stereotypes can persist because men are able to determine the definitions used. Where male experience is the norm, women's behaviour can be classified as deviant. The key point is that men have power. It is, as Eichler notes, irrelevant 'whether the claim made is that women are inferior, superior, or different but equal, since it is strictly a matter of power who decrees what is a criterion of inferiority, superiority, or essential equivalence.'[2] The common link between the microinequities of sexism in children's books, through sexual harassment and violence against women, is the sense that men own the world, and have the right to dominate it. The challenge of feminism is the insistence that women have as much right to act in and influence the world as do men, and must be treated equally in relationships. This has to be taken on board by men, especially in a Church which has for so long reinforced ideas of male superiority.

All that has been said here points to the urgent need for Christians to address the wider issues of what is happening between the sexes. Yet Christian thinking about sexual ethics still concentrates much more on who has the right to do what to whom, than on the content of a relationship. One way of combatting sexual violence is to expand our thinking about sexual ethics. Marie Fortune has suggested that we ought to speak of an ethic based on mutual consent rather than coercion. Sexual activity with children will always be wrong according to this criterion, for children can never give free, informed consent. Adult-child sexual contact is unacceptable because it is nonconsensual and exploitative, not because it is sexual: 'Sexual ethics need to deal more directly with issues of consent and power, and with the potential for exploitation and abuse.' The guiding principle must be, 'Thou shalt not sexually manipulate, take advantage of, or abuse another person at any time.'

This means that people must learn not to act on all sexual feelings, where there is not consent, or it is inappropriate. This does not mean that couples may not try to persuade each other to have sex. But couples who care for each other will respect the other's desires, and be prepared to take no for an answer. The same ethic applies within marriage as without, for 'Marriage does not make forced sexual intercourse "sex" rather than rape.'[3] Paul's idea that wife and husband should rule over each other's bodies can be taken as an encouragement towards mutuality with regard to sex. Following that might enable us to move away from our current male-centred perspective on sex, which makes the male orgasm in intercourse the central, or even only, activity.

If it is accepted that an ethic of consent is important, this makes a difference to how sex education is carried out. In the view of many people, including many Christians, knowledge of sex and sexuality should be kept for marriage. Sex education for them is a question of giving some practical information about reproduction, whilst urging teenagers to keep their sexual feelings under control. The public acknowledgement of child sexual abuse has meant some changes in the way we talk to children about their bodies. Even very small children are encouraged to see that they have a right to bodily integrity, and should in their turn respect that of others. As Fortune points out, providing 'teenagers with information and the sense that sex is a gift from God intended to be shared responsibly in relationship to another is one of the most effective means of *preventing* sexual abuse and sexual violence.'[4]

Rousseau and Gallagher discuss the need for parents to be open with their children about sex, both because their commitment to each other helps their children to feel loved and accepted, and because it offers a good model. We must tell them, say Rousseau and Gallagher, 'what it feels like to be close to someone, what are some of the things we do to make each other feel especially loved and cherished, and what we especially delight in about each other.'[5]

Making consent an important criterion does not imply the abandonment of the traditional Christian belief that sexual intercourse properly belongs in marriage. But it may lead us to rethink why Christians hold this belief. Our attention needs to be focused more on the quality of sexual relationships, not simply on where they take place. Veronica Zundel laments the nature of the advice offered to mature single people about sexuality, noting ironically that 'advice designed to keep impressionable teenagers out of bed becomes increasingly inadequate for the more mature', for example the single mother with children, or the new convert who has had many sexual partners.[6] A stress on the importance of keeping yourself pure for marriage, and for the one right person, does not address their situations.

A number of theologians have explored the reasons for keeping sex for marriage. Jack Dominian has written at length on this, and John Spong emphasizes the importance of commitment: 'The highest development of human character and the greatest potential joy are finally the results and by-products of the total commitment of one person to another in a holy marriage.' 'Nothing', he says, 'can open life to the depths of love, to the discovery of those hidden wells of personhood, more than a commitment intended for a lifetime in which two persons agree to share themselves fully and freely with each other and to grow together for all of their days.'[7] What we may need to move away from is the notion that sexual sins exist in isolation from other manifestations of human brokenness. It is wrong to lie, cheat, hurt others, and to devalue ourselves, whether we do that through sexual means or in other ways. Our sexuality is a major element in the way we relate to other people, and that is why it is important to behave with integrity sexually.

At the heart of the ethic of consent is the idea that the other person is a subject in their own right, whose point of view matters. And this is the criterion against which we judge pornography and dismissive attitudes towards women. What lies behind these is, as Kappeler shows, the way men see women as objects rather than subjects with their own individuality. Women are there to support and service men, and keep themselves in the background when not required. What they are not to do is to have an independent life of their own, either doing without men or forcing their needs or viewpoints on men. The ethic of consent suggests that on an individual level, both the man and the woman have an equal right to having their needs met and their points of view heard. On a wider level, it means that women must be able to participate in the democratic processes of Church and state, and be able to shape culture in the way men have done. Some parts of the Church have drawn up equal opportunities policies, and this is to be welcomed. But such policies can only be pursued effectively if serious attention is given to what has gone wrong between the sexes.

That process will not be painless, and the difficulties will be particularly acute for men. It means acknowledging that the sex to which they belong has done wrong in oppressing women, and that even men who support feminism have benefited from this. And it means a commitment to opposing discrimination and negative attitudes towards women in both public and private spheres. Current ideas about masculinity do hurt men, but for men to concentrate merely on expressing their feelings and healing their own pain is to avoid the issue of their power. Harry Brod points out that male pain is the underside of male power, and though there is a cost to men it is not the same as the cost to women. Emotional restraint confers power, he says; witholding personal information and appearing rational, allow men to get the upper hand: 'Men adopt self-destructive behaviours not because they are evil or stupid, but because society makes it appear in their interests to do so, by conferring very real power on those who conform to these norms.' Brod concludes that 'the only way to gain the capacity to heal male pain is to incapacitate male power.'[8] Yet asking men to relinquish their power will feel like a threat to their very identity, perhaps even their Christian identity.

For Christian thinking about men's role in society has overwhelmingly accepted that men should be in control – of themselves, of women and of the world. Christians may speak of men being under the lordship of Christ, but otherwise this view closely parallels what *most* men think masculinity is all about. Hite found that men defined being a man as being self-assured, unafraid, in control and autonomous, not dependent, and showing leadership or dominance.[9] It is important for Christian men to look at the extent to which Christianity has sanctioned this view of masculinity, with little attempt to make a critique of it. Hite's work clearly reveals the strains this puts on men, and the same must be true within the Church. For all our sakes, we need to challenge men about their need to feel in control, and the way we speak of God can help in this. Too often we talk only of the heavy responsibility God lays on men to work hard and lead wisely. Instead we might emphasize the disturbing spontaneity of the Holy Spirit, and the way that God works through weakness and subverts traditional masculine values.

But where do women fit into this? Are men to be left alone to work on their problems, or to be supported – with the danger that women once again focus all their energies on men's concerns? Pure feminist principles might suggest that men must fight the battle against male power on their own. Yet this is unrealistic, since, as Wise and Stanley point out:

One consequence of women changing is that we change the social circumstances within which men live, so that they get edged and pushed, even nudged, to the point where they have to begin to change or to openly resist. In other words, whatever happens it will be women who make it happen, whether directly in our own lives or indirectly in the lives of men.[10]

Most pro-feminist men have probably come to that viewpoint through the influence of women, and will continue to need some support from women. But it is important for men to try to explore personal issues with other men, rather than relying on women. As Rosalind Coward observes, it is not a good sign for a man to prefer women as friends because of the depth women can offer. For this feeling is 'generated by men splitting off their emotions – seeking out men for one kind of strangely impersonal bonding and women for the hard work of intimate and sustained personal friendship.'[11]

Christian women, however horrified they are at the extent of male abuse of women, will want to hold on to the fact that men are their brothers. After all, Christianity requires that we love even our enemies with a genuine and all-encompassing love, and even if women think of men in general as an enemy, most love at least some individual men. Christians have to reckon with the fact that everybody matters, and that we cannot write off whole groups of people. Helen Oppenheimer makes the point that we should think in terms of the irreplaceability of persons, whatever they are like or have done:

> Everyone can agree that Michelangelo is irreplaceable, but when God says of a drunken tramp, 'But I loved that one. I did not want him lost,' God's other children must try to see the point. We should see it, after all, if the tramp's human mother said it. What the belief in a heavenly Father requires is the exercise of imagination to see each other's irreplaceability.[12]

Men and women matter as unique individuals. It is possible to face the fact of male oppression of women squarely, and not deny it in the interests of false harmony, because it *matters* that men are like that. Recognizing that men are not created to be tyrants is the first step in working for change.

Women and men need to work together not only because

we need to respect each other's uniqueness, but because interdependence is of vital importance. It might be argued that the human need for relationships can be met by relating entirely to one's own sex. But a deliberate refusal to relate to the other sex falls into the trap of stereotyping them, and failing to see their individuality. Moreover, we learn from each other as women and men, not because we are by nature totally different creatures, but because our experiences (influenced by our biology) are different.

It is in marriage and close sexual relationships that we are most likely to be relating closely to the other sex. Yet we need other friendships and acquaintanceships too, with both men and women, if we are to grow to understand one another. Unfortunately, such friendships can slide into inappropriate sexual relationships, and that is why Christians are sometimes warned against having close friendships with someone of the other sex. James Nelson pinpoints this dilemma when he writes, 'In the goodness of our sexuality and our created eros we reach out for each other. But in the woundedness and distortions of our sexuality, our capacity for friendship depends on the grace of redemption.'[13]

Part of the problem may be that there is no well-defined social role for such friends, particularly if they are married. Perhaps the model ought to be that of good family relationships, where there is a recognition of the other's sexuality, but agreement that it would be inappropriate to behave sexually with each other. Given the suspicions and jealousies and occasional lapses which are generated when women and men develop friendships, it is understandable that some think it too dangerous to pursue them. Heterosexual men and women may feel more at ease if they think their partner's colleagues at work are of the same sex. Yet must we think that where women and men work together, there will inevitably either be physical sexual relationships or a relentless battle against temptation?

It is, paradoxically, the ability to be fully sexual beings which helps to liberate us from sexual sin. Those who are afraid of their sexuality, or see it as a loathsome appetite which must be kept under control at all costs, magnify the sexual element in all relationships way out of proportion. Those who are happy with their sexuality find it enhances their relationships without leading to inappropriate physical expression. This is true in the celibate life at its best. Rousseau and Gallagher argue that since we are called to love our neighbours with our whole selves, 'Any whole and healthy love . . . any love given by any one person to any other person, is going to be sexual love in some sense.' Human beings cannot love without sexual passion. 'When we try to eliminate or repress our sexual feelings,' they say, 'we inhibit our love. And inhibited love is not the kind that brings about our intimacy with God.'[14] This seems far removed from the world of pornography, innuendo, sexual harassment and violence, and unsatisfying sexual encounters. Yet perhaps that model of uninhibited and passionate love is one which desperately needs to be promoted amongst Christians.

White Western Christians at least seem to have so many problems about their bodies, to have lost the joy of physicality and createdness. This leads to a stunted existence, and not the living and loving God intends for us. The hymn writer quoted at the start of this chapter sees the Spirit of God as giving love blended with passion, and pleasure that can never cloy. We need to recapture these elements, not as merely spiritual qualities, but as sanctified physical enjoyment of the world. My upbringing was in a church where we changed 'catholic' to 'universal' in the creed to avoid any hint of papacy, and there was a corresponding dismissal of candles, vestments, incense and the like. Yet churches in that tradition miss out by failing to recognize the goodness of our bodies, and that worship of God can be expressed through smell, touch, taste, hearing and sight. In practice, catholic churches may mystify the sacraments out of the ordinary world, yet essentially they are about bodiliness.

It may be that the Christian faith, rightly understood, could help us to integrate our bodiliness and our sexuality with the rest of our lives. This seems to be a problem which men have, though most might not recognize it as such. It is important for all of us to understand that

> sexuality is far more than genital activity. It is our way of being in the world as gendered persons, having male or female biological structures and socially internalized self-understandings of those meanings to us. Sexuality means having feelings and attitudes about being 'body-selves' ... It means having the capacity for sensuousness.[15]

Perhaps we can think of sexuality as being as much a part of ourselves as our thinking. Both are integral and connected parts of being human which we cannot 'turn off', but we have some choice about how both are expressed.

We are to bring our whole selves to our work, our leisure and our relationships, not allow ourselves to compartmentalize our sexuality, or our ability to think or care. Life may feel less complicated when we partition it off. For example, we may only feel able to cope with a difficult job if we can put it out of our minds while we are at home. Yet this creates its own stress within ourselves and for those with whom we live. We may also use our jobs to escape from family demands. This may be a life-saver for those who have stressful family lives, and it may give them fresh energy to cope. Yet it is counter-productive if workers alienate themselves from their families through continual absence, and many men fall into this trap.

It might help if it were more publicly recognized that male workers are often also fathers, and may need to have some flexibility so as to combine these different roles. Yet as Moss and Fonda point out:

> Working mothers, or indeed working fathers, are not *the problem*. That lies in the failure of family life, work life and society in general to have yet developed the means to enable these roles to be comfortably combined, without penalizing one or more of the participants, be it fathers, mothers, children or employers.[16]

Some attention needs to be given here to employment practices in the Church. For despite the progress that has been made in training and ministry, minister's families are often still expected to have a very low priority.

It is important to recognize the interconnections between the spheres of home and work, public and private. The acknowledgement that there are not rigidly separate masculine and feminine realms may help women and men to see more clearly what each has in common, rather than regarding the other sex as opposite and 'other'. This has an impact, too, on our knowledge of God; for we learn to see that God is concerned with the whole of life, and every aspect of our experience. The fact that we cannot polarize masculinity and femininity as opposite 'principles', reflects the God in whose image both sexes are made.

Yet whatever the ideal, we must take seriously the present degree of alienation between the sexes; it is not enough simply to assert their equality before God. Centuries of patriarchy are not overcome by good intention, and we must face up to the deep-rooted misogyny at the heart of our culture and our churches. Male domination within the Church has been justified by a whole edifice of theological assumptions about the necessity of the Godhead being spoken about and represented only in male terms. Acceptance of discrimination against women is enshrined both in Church legislation and in the hearts of many Christians. It is true that many Christians do accept the principle of the equality of the sexes. Some also recognize that the demands of justice entail special measures to oppose the oppression of women. But few churches actively try to reform relationships between the sexes or to transform social systems, and our witness in the world is seriously damaged as a consequence. I am tired of having to apologize for belonging to the Church, because others see it as such a reactionary organization.

I write at the start of a Decade of Evangelism. If only the main thrust of this could be the invitation to meet a God who is on the side of the disadvantaged and oppressed, and who liberates us from our distorted attitudes to sexuality and to each other. The *Faith in the City* report side-stepped the question of women in the Church, but it rightly proclaimed:

It is only when the church itself is sensed to be a community in which all alienation caused by age, gender, race and class is decisively overcome that its mission can begin to be authentic among the millions who feel themselves alienated, not only from the church, but from society as a whole.[17]

It is often said that the years of discussion in the Church of England about women priests have distracted it from its true task of mission. But that mission cannot be carried out effectively whilst we continue to demonstrate such a stunted model of sexuality and relationships between the sexes.

To suggest that such a deep-rooted problem can be ended just by individual men and women being nicer to each other is to lay ourselves open to Jeremiah's charge: 'They have healed the wound of my people lightly, saying, "Peace, peace," when there is no peace' (Jer. 6.14). The same charge must be applied to those Christians who put forward 'the Family' and traditional values as the way to bring peace in society. It is within families and the traditional order that many people, especially women, have suffered, and those wounds must not be treated lightly. At the same time, it is quite wrong for Christians to speak of respecting women and their role in the family whilst in fact treating them as weak and dependent. Neither veneration of women as saints or mothers, nor good-humoured tolerance of ladies' little ways, belong in the Christian community; only respect and understanding based on our shared humanity and imaging of God.

We appreciate the scale of the problem more when we name patriarchy as one of the principalities and powers against which Christians must struggle (Eph. 6.12). Yet, whatever force of evil might be said to inspire such systems, they are nonetheless human. Dworkin has a point: 'There are no disembodied processes . . . all history originates in human flesh . . . all oppression is inflicted by the body of one against the body of another . . . all social change is built on the bone and muscle, and out of the flesh and blood, of human creators.'[18] If it is a human system, then it can be transformed, for without our co-operation it must begin to fall.

I began this book by pointing out that there are two ways of viewing women's situation, causes for hope as well as for pessimism. The sheer extent of negative attitudes towards women feels overwhelming, particularly when it is encountered in the christian community; yet there are now many individuals and groups who share the vision of a different world, and are working for change. The Christian faith offers us the theological virtue of hope, which forbids defeatism. Our knowledge that it is only in the new order of the Kingdom of God that this and all other oppressions will ultimately be overcome gives us hope, while it also puts our efforts into perspective. The difficulties we face do not relieve us from our calling. Indeed, it is inevitable that the new ways of living we work for will bring with them their own new problems. Much is laid at the door of feminism – marriage breakdown and delinquency as well as an increase in male violence. Such claims are exaggerated, and yet it must be admitted that new freedoms for women do disturb the status quo. There is a price to pay for any advance, whether of science or political freedoms. One important contribution Christianity can make is to remind us of the existence of sin and evil, which prevent our establishing any earthly utopia.

It is vital that Christians draw up a serious critique of the way masculinity is defined in our society, and of the distorted relationships between the sexes. At the moment we view each other through lenses that give only distorted images; we need to see more clearly. My hope is that by drawing the attention of Christians to these issues, we can begin to do our part in restoring our shared image in God.

Notes

1 THE WRONGS OF WOMANKIND

1. Tertullian, quoted in D. Pape, *God and Women: A Fresh Look at What the New Testament says about Women* (Oxford, Mowbray, 1977), p. 181.
2. Elizabeth Cady Stanton, who had five sons, quoted in A. Rich, *Of Woman Born* (London, Virago; New York, Bantam Books, 1977), p. 206.
3. I use the term 'patriarchy' to cover the *system* of male domination, and 'sexism' for particular instances of discrimination against women.
4. See the section on 'Men and Society' in Further Reading, below.
5. *Observer*, 6 January 1985.
6. See S. Witherspoon, 'Interim report: A woman's work', in *British Social Attitudes 1988/9*.
7. J. Seager and A. Olson, *Women in the World* (London, Pan; New York, Simon and Schuster, 1986), p. 7. There are two types of female circumcision. In the 'milder' form, excision, all or part of the clitoris and sometimes the internal vaginal lips are removed. In the other, all the external genitalia are removed and the outer vaginal lips sewn shut, leaving only a tiny opening for urine and menstrual blood.
8. D. Taylor et al., *Women: A World Report* (London, Methuen, 1985) illustrates this, and there is a growing amount of material available by women from many different countries, including women's theology. See, for example, Elsa Tamez, ed., *Through Her Eyes: Women's Theology from Latin America* (New York, Orbis Books, 1989) and L. Russell, K. Pui-Lan, A. Isasi-Diaz and K. Cannon, eds, *Inheriting Our Mothers' Gardens: Feminist Theology in Third World Perspective* (Philadelphia, Westminster, 1988). In Britain, the women's movement has strong trade union and working-class links.
9. A Dworkin, *Right-Wing Women* (London, Women's Press; New York, Putnam Publishing Group, 1983), p. 217.
10. Mary Rowe speaking of harassment, quoted in M. Pellauer, B. Chester and J. Boyajian, eds, *Sexual Assault and Abuse* (New York, Harper & Row, 1987), p. 164.
11. I explored the effects and meaning of women's idealization in *A Woman's Work*, London, SPCK, 1989.
12. J. Brown and R. Parker in J. Brown and C. Bohn, eds, *Christianity, Patriarchy and Abuse* (New York, The Pilgrim's Press, 1989), p. 3.
13. R. R. Ruether, *Sexism and God-Talk: Toward a Feminist Theology* (London, SCM; Boston, Beacon, 1984), pp. 191-2.

2 NEVERTHELESS A WOMAN

1. M. Mead, quoted in D. Spender, *Men's Studies Modified* (Oxford and Elmsford, NY, Pergamon, 1981), p. 1.
2. M. Luther, quoted in J. Bussert, *Battered Women* (Lutheran Church in America, 1986), p. 10.
3. J. Morley in M. Furlong, ed., *Feminine in the Church* (London, SPCK, 1984), p. 60.
4. P. G. Wodehouse, *Heavy Weather*. London, Penguin 1979.
5. C. Gilman, quoted in D. Spender, *Man-Made Language* (London and Boston, Routledge & Kegan Paul, 1980), pp. 145-6.
6. See for example, K. Barth, *Church Dogmatics* III, 1 (Edinburgh, T. & T. Clark, 1986), pp. 308-9, and S. Clark, *Man and Woman in Christ* (Edinburgh, T. & T. Clark; Ann Arbor, MI, Servant Books, 1980), pp. 13n, 25.
7. Russell et al., *Inheriting Our Mothers' Gardens*, pp. 76ff.
8. Letter to *Newstand* (a Methodist paper), 1985.
9. M. Korda, *Male Chauvinism!* (London, Hodder & Stoughton, 1975; New York, Ballantine Books, 1979), p. 165.
10. A. Oakley, *Women Confined*. London, Martin Robertson, 1980.
11. R. Deem, *Schooling for Women's Work* (London and Boston, Routledge & Kegan Paul, 1980), p. 29.
12. Rudolph Bell explores the links between anorexics and saints who starved themselves in *Holy Anorexia* (Chicago, University of Chicago Press, 1985), and Sara Maitland writes of masochism and female saints in L. Hurcombe, ed., *Sex and God* (London, Routledge & Kegan Paul; New York, Routledge, Chapman and Hall, 1987).
13. A. Dickson, *A Woman in Your Own Right* (London, Quartet, 1982), and F. Dewar, *Live for a Change* (London, Darton, Longman & Todd, 1988). Feminist explorations of spirituality often makes these connections explicit.
14. P. Shuttle and P. Redgrove, *Wise Wound: Menstruation and Everywoman* (London, Gollancz; New York, Richard Marek Pubs, 1978). See also E. Martin, *The Woman in the Body*, Milton Keynes, Open University Press; Boston, Beacon Press, 1987.
15. Reproduced by kind permission of Frances Croake Frank.
16. The Church of England Report *Ageing* (London, Church House Publishing, 1990) makes some important points about valuing older people, and recognizes the issue of gender. Its practical recommendations are worth taking up.
17. J. Hearn and W. Parkin, *Sex at Work* (Hemel Hempstead, Herts, Wheatsheaf, 1987), p. 141.

Notes

1. Cato, quoted in Bussert, *Battered Women*, p. 18.
2. D. H. Lawrence, quoted in L. Russell, *Human Liberation in a Feminist Perspective* (Philadelphia, Westminster Press, 1974), p. 148.
3. There is an excellent discussion of this point in J. R. Richards, *The Sceptical Feminist* (London and Boston, Routledge & Kegan Paul, 1980); for a general discussion of sex differences, see J. Nicholson, *Men and Women* (Oxford, Oxford University Press, 1984).
4. Korda, *Male Chauvinism*, pp. 3-4. This is borne out in studies of men, for example, S. Hite, *The Hite Report on Male Sexuality*, London, Macdonald; New York, Knopf, 1981; A. Ford, *Men*, London, Weidenfeld & Nicolson, 1985; M. Ingham, *Men*, London, Century, 1984.
5. Ford, *Men*, p. 101.
6. See V. Woolf, *A Room of One's Own/Three Guineas* (London, Chatto & Windus, 1984), and here, p. 37.
7. Korda, *Male Chauvinism*, p. 148.
8. Ruether, *Sexism and God-Talk*, p. 168.
9. C. Osborne, in J. Petersen, ed., *For Men Only* (Wheaton, IL, Tyndale House, 1982), p. 79.
10. Rich, *Of Woman Born*, p. 11.
11. D. Dinnerstein, *The Rocking of the Cradle* (London, Souvenir Press, 1976), pp. 161, 173.
12. J. Bernard, *The Future of Marriage* (London, Souvenir Press; New York, Bantam Books, 1973), p. 18.
13. Susanne Kappeler, drawing on John Berger's work, develops the idea that man sees woman in a similar way to that in which 'man' is said to see animals. Man puts his own meanings on the other, but is not looking for an encounter, and does not see himself from the other's viewpoint. Though fond of woman or animal, he has a power of disposal over this other's life. S. Kappeler, *Pornography and Representation* (Cambridge, Polity Press, 1986), ch. 6.
14. G. Greer, *The Female Eunuch* (London, MacGibbon & Kee; New York, McGraw-Hill, 1971), p. 249.
15. Elisabeth Schüssler Fiorenza attempts to come to terms with the reality of women's situation in the New Testament in *In Memory of Her* (London, SCM; New York, Crossroad, 1984), see especially ch. 1.
16. Ruether, *Sexism and God-Talk*, p. 80.
17. E. Strachan and G. Strachan, *Freeing the Feminine* (Laburnam Publications 1985), p. 125.
18. Though it should be said that even in cultures which do not see the world dualistically, men and women do not relate equally.
19. R. McCloughry, 'Real Men', *Third Way*, vol. 12, no. 9, pp. 6-8.
20. See A. Campbell, *The Gospel of Anger*, London, SPCK, 1986.
21. Korda, *Male Chauvinism*, p. 47.

22. Quoted in Pape, *God and Women*, p. 179.
23. Richard Harries, Oxford Diocesan letter, Summer 1989.

4 'MEN, WHO NEEDS THEM?'

1. S. Hite, *Women and Love* (London, Viking; New York, St Martin's Press, 1989), p. 695.
2. N. Morton, in A. Hageman, ed., *Sexist Religion and Women in the Church* (New York, Association Press, 1974), p. 30.
3. Quoted in Pape, *God and Women*, p. 142.
4. P. Plattner in Petersen, *For Men Only*, p. 64. It is tempting to add that it is that kind of separation of emotion from work which enables a man to sit in a bunker prepared to bring about the destruction of the earth, and then go home to his wife and child, saying, 'Of course I'd push the button . . . I try not to think about it in personal terms.'
5. J. Nicholson, *A Question of Sex* (London, Fontana, 1979), p. 92 (republished as *Men and Women*, New York, Oxford University Press, 1984).
6. M. Mead, *Male and Female* (London, Penguin, 1971), p. 286.
7. N. Chodorow, *The Reproduction of Mothering* (Berkeley, CA, University of California Press, 1978), p. 181.
8. Ingham, *Men*, p. 113.
9. A. Bridges in Petersen, *For Men Only*, p. 99.
10. David Augsburger, ibid., pp. 56-7.
11. J. Inkpen, 'Tender Comrade', *Southwell and Oxford Papers on Contemporary Society*, December 1989. See also B. Wren, *What Language Should I Borrow?* (London, SCM; New York, Crossroad, 1989), especially ch. 7, 'A Male for Others'.
12. J. Nelson, *The Intimate Connection* (Philadelphia, Westminster, 1988), quotations from pp. 45, 21 and 35. Now that this issue has been raised, we may well see more contributions from men in this area.
13. Woolf, *A Room of One's Own*, pp. 35-6.
14. Nelson, *The Intimate Connection*, p. 53. Hite's work on male sexuality illustrates the extent to which performance anxiety pervades men's sexual relationships.
15. S. Sharpe, *Just Like a Girl* (London, Penguin, 1976), p. 219.
16. B. Ehrenreich, *The Hearts of Men* (London, Pluto Press, 1985; New York, Doubleday, 1984), p. 149ff.
17. Korda, *Male Chauvinism*, p. 222.
18. Rich, *Of Woman Born*, p. 214.

5 WHERE WOMEN DON'T BELONG

1. Sir Humphrey Appleby (of BBC TV's *Yes Minister*), quoted in R. Miles, *Women and Power* (London, Macdonald, 1985), p. 73.

2. Korda, *Male Chauvinism*, paraphrased from p. 63.
3. P. Willis, *Learning to Labour* (London, Saxon House; Lexington, MA, Lexington Books, 1977), p. 150.
4. B. Rogers, *Men Only* (London, Pandora, 1988), and C. Cooper and M. Davidson, *High Pressure* (London, Fontana, 1982).
5. See, for example, J. Finch, *Married to the Job* (London and Winchester, MA, George Allen & Unwin, 1983), and C. Piotrkowski, *Work and the Family System* (New York, The Free Press, 1978).
6. B. Jackson, *Fatherhood* (London, George Allen & Unwin, 1983), p. 118.
7. I pointed to some reasons for this in *A Woman's Work*. Mary Ann Coates's book *Clergy Stress* (London, SPCK, 1989), is a fuller study.
8. Korda, *Male Chauvinism*, p. 86.
9. J. S. Mill, quoted in Richards, *The Sceptical Feminist*, p. 101.
10. Mead, *Male and Female*, p. 339.
11. S. Wise and L. Stanley, *Georgie Porgie* (London, Pandora, 1987), pp. 39-41 and 61.
12. Hearn and Parkin, *Sex at Work*, p. 85.
13. L. Segal, *Is the Future Female?* (London, Virago, 1987; New York, Peter Bedrick Books, 1988), p. 187ff.
14. N. Lawson, reviewing *Misogynies*, *The Times*, 20 April 1989.
15. See, for example, S. Westwood, *All Day Every Day* (London, Pluto, 1984; Champaign, University of Illinois Press, 1985). Though rare, it is not unknown for women to harass other women sexually.
16. Miles, *Women and Power*, p. 122.
17. This version is taken from R. Dawson, *And All that is Unseen* (London, Church House Publishing, 1986), p. 39.
18. Cooper and Davidson, *High Pressure*, p. 58.

6 DAMAGED RELATIONSHIPS

1. Dinnerstein, *The Rocking of the Cradle*, p. 276.
2. Ruether, *Sexism and God-Talk*, p. 161.
3. Some of the evidence is suggestive, however, and research continues to uncover new facts about women's role in early societies. The classic texts outlining theories about matriarchy include J. Bachofen, *Myth, Religion and Mother Right* (Princeton University Press, 1973); E. Gould Davis, *The First Sex* (London, Penguin, 1972); and M. Stone, *When God was a Woman* (New York, The Dial Press, 1976).
4. J. Hick, *Evil and the God of Love* (London, Macmillan; New York, Harper & Row, 1977), p. 300.
5. P. Trible, *God and the Rhetoric of Sexuality* (Philadelphia, Fortress, 1978), p. 128.
6. Hite, *Women and Love*, pp. 56 and 72.
7. H. Brod, ed., *A Mensch among Men* (Freedom, CA, The Crossing Press, 1988), p. 10.

8. Kimmel, in Brod, *A Mensch among Men*, p. 155.
9. Hite, *Women and Love*, pp. 122 and 135.
10. Hite, *Women and Love*, p. 142.
11. Ford, *Men*, pp. 36 and 46. See also Ingham, *Men*. It is possible that the work of Hite, Ford and Ingham is slanted by the fact that all are women, though all include lengthy interviews in which men speak for themselves. Hite also operated a control group in which men thought they were being surveyed by a man. The range of men Hite interviewed closely matched the range of men in the United States population at large.
12. J. Dobson, *Man to Man About Women* (Eastbourne, Kingsway, 1976), p. 96.
13. V. Zundel, 'Carbon Dating', *Third Way*, vol. 13, no. 1, pp. 16-18.
14. A. Schaef, *When Society Becomes an Addict* (New York, Harper & Row, 1988), pp. 40 and 22-3.
15. M. French, *Beyond Power* (London, Cape; New York, Ballantine Books, 1986), pp. 85-6 and 136.
16. J. Morley, Chrysalis, July 1989; J. Morley, *All Desires Known* (London, MOW/WIT, 1988; Wilton, CN, Morehouse, 1989).
17. J. Williams in Furlong, *Feminine in the Church*, p. 98.
18. P. Clark in Furlong, *Feminine in the Church*, p. 186.
19. Ruether, *Sexism and God-Talk*, pp. 188-9 and 231.

7 STORMY PASSIONS

1. Nineteenth-century evangelist Billy Sunday, beginning a sermon, quoted in Bussert, *Battered Women*, p. 56.
2. M. Rousseau and C. Gallagher, *Sex Is Holy* (New York, Amity House, 1986), p. 23.
3. Nelson suggests that Paul does not usually mean sensuality by 'sarx', or 'the flesh', but attempts to save ourselves by our own works (*The Intimate Connection*, p. 24). Yet the word is commonly understood by Christians as applying to our physicality, and thus the damage is done.
4. J. Nelson, *Embodiment* (Minneapolis, MN, Augsburg, 1978), p. 71.
5. E. Mueller, letter to *Leadership Today*, January 1988.
6. Swindoll, in *Leadership Today*, November 1987.
7. Segal, *Is the Future Female?*, p. 92.
8. See H. Terry, 'Prostitutes — losers in the game', *Third Way*, vol. 9, no. 10, pp. 10-12, for a sympathetic Christian approach to prostitutes.
9. Hite, *The Hite Report on Male Sexuality*, p. 760. Hite points out that though many men resent women's emotional and economic dependence, they fail to see this as a problem of inequality in society, instead blaming their own wife for behaving unreasonably.
10. Ford, *Men*, p. 164.
11. D. Cameron and E. Frazer, *The Lust to Kill* (Cambridge, Polity Press; New York University Press, 1987), p. 169.

12. M. Fortune, *Sexual Violence* (New York, Pilgrim Press, 1983), p. 20.
13. Plattner, in Petersen, *For Men Only*, p. 66ff.
14. Taylor, ibid., p. 49.
15. T. Bovet, ibid., pp. 58-9.
16. Rousseau and Gallagher, *Sex is Holy*, p. 17.
17. *Leadership Today*, November 1987.
18. Rousseau and Gallagher, *Sex is Holy*, pp. 109 and 62.
19. Hite, *The Hite Report on Male Sexuality*, see especially pp. 477ff.
20. Ingham, *Men*, p. 150.
21. D. Lodge, *Nice Work*, London and New York, Penguin, 1989.
22. R. Coward, *Female Desires* (London, Paladin; New York, Grove Press, 1985), p. 192.
23. E. E. Morgan, 'The Eroticization of Male Dominance', *Michigan Papers in Women's Studies* (vol. 11, no. 1, Sept. 1975), pp. 130-1.
24. See, for example, S. Jeffreys, *Anticlimax* (London, Women's Press, 1990).

8 A CHEAP WAY TO BUY A WOMAN

1. A respondent quoted in Hite, *The Hite Report on Male Sexuality*, p. 777.
2. R. Dawkins, *The Selfish Gene* (Oxford and New York, Oxford University Press, 1989), p. 5.
3. F. Catherwood, quoted in H. Terry, 'And women shall be silent: the meaning of pornography', *Third Way*, vol. 11, no. 3, pp. 20-2.
4. Fortune, *Sexual Violence*, p. 232.
5. Kappeler, *Pornography and Representation*, p. 101ff.
6. C. Itzin in G. Chester and J. Dickey, eds, *Feminism and Censorship* (Bridport, Dorset, Prism Press, 1988), pp. 39-40.
7. *Cosmopolitan*, March 1990. In this chapter I am concentrating on heterosexual pornographic material, which is the major part of the market, and which contributes to the distorted relationships between the sexes. Porn produced for gay men demeans men in similar ways, but I do not discuss it here. The question of whether lesbian pornography also demeans women is currently the subject of heated debate in feminist circles.
8. M. Baxter, 'Flesh and Blood', *New Scientist*, 5 May 1990.
9. *Observer*, 16 April 1989.
10. E. Carola in Chester and Dickey, *Feminism and Censorship*, p. 177.
11. *Feminism and Censorship* includes a range of viewpoints view on this.
12. *Observer*, 16 April 1989.
13. C. Lee, *The Ostrich Position* (London, Unwin; New York, Writers & Readers, 1986), p. 75. See also the same author's *Friday's Child* (Wellingborough, Thorsons, 1988).

14. BBC Radio 4 report, 'From Our Own Correspondent', 12 May 1990.
15. Rousseau and Gallagher, *Sex is Holy*, p. 115.
16. J. Reeves, *For Better, For Worse?* (London, Triangle, 1986), p. 96f.
17. One could debate whether this is a saying applicable to both sexes, or specifically directed at men; but many Christians would feel it applied in the situation I have described.
18. For an investigation of this, see S. Griffin, *Pornography and Silence* (London, Women's Press; New York, Harper & Row, 1981).
19. *Observer*, 16 April 1989. See Jeffreys, *Anticlimax*, for a recent critique of how pornography has been justified.
20. Hite, *The Hite Report on Male Sexuality*, ch. 6.
21. Segal, *Is the Future Female?*, pp. 107-8.
22. Coward, *Female Desires*, p. 102.
23. Griffin, *Pornography and Silence*, p. 3.
24. Lee, *The Ostrich Position*, pp. 141ff.
25. *The Tablet*, 27 May 1989.
26. Terry, 'And Women shall be silent'.
27. Kappeler, *Pornography and Representation*, pp. 40f. and 60f.

9 SEXUAL VIOLENCE

1. Macauly (1957), quoted in E. Wilson, *Only Halfway to Paradise* (London, Tavistock; New York, Methuen, 1980), p. 93.
2. Pellauer et al., *Sexual Assault and Abuse*, p. 7.
3. Wise and Stanley, *Georgie Porgie*, p. 90.
4. L. Kelly, *Surviving Sexual Violence* (Cambridge, Polity Press; Minneapolis, University of Minnesota Press, 1988), p. 97.
5. Cameron and Fraser, *The Lust to Kill*, p. 164.
6. ibid., pp. 171ff. See also Jeffreys, *Anticlimax*.
7. Hite, *The Hite Report on Male Sexuality*, pp. 711ff.
8. *Oxford Courier*, 3 May 1990.
9. Pellauer et al., *Sexual Assault and Abuse*, p. 86.
10. Fortune, *Sexual Violence*, pp. 7-8.
11. Pellauer et al., *Sexual Assault and Abuse*, p. 147.
12. J. Saward, *Rape — My Story*. London, Bloomsbury, 1990.
13. ibid., p. 46.
14. Fortune, *Sexual Violence*, pp. 177ff.
15. Reproduced by permission from Kelly, *Surviving Sexual Violence*, pp. 35-6.
16. It has been estimated that only around 2 per cent of rape reports are false. Pellauer, op. cit., p. 5.
17. ibid., pp. 117f.
18. Cf. the use in pornography of settings in nurses' homes or convents. Wise and Stanley in *Georgie Porgie* describe the challenge their lesbianism seemed to present to men.

10 HOME IS WHERE THE HURT IS

1. A pastor speaking to a battered woman, quoted in Bussert, *Battered Women*, p. 64.
2. Council of Toledo, quoted in Bussert, *Battered Women*, p. 12.
3. Adam Jukes, *Observer*, 25 February 1990.
4. Bussert, *Battered Women*, p. 61.
5. A. Horton and J. Williamson, *Abuse and Religion* (Lexington, MA, Lexington Books, 1988), p. 53.
6. I do not know whether police treat domestic violence between males in the same way. Is it that the *home* is seen as private, or simply a matter of gender?
7. This information is taken from Bussert, *Battered Women*, and Horton and Williamson, *Abuse and Religion*. Elder abuse has been a hidden problem which is beginning to come to light at the time of writing.
8. This and subsequent points are made in 'Wifebeaters', *Observer*, 25 February 1990.
9. Leacock, in M. Lowe and R. Hubbard, eds, *Woman's Nature* (Oxford and Elmsford, NY, Pergamon Press, 1983), p. 113.
10. Bussert, *Battered Women*, p. 42.
11. *Faith in the City* (London, Church House Publishing, 1985), p. 282. Helena Terry outlines a Christian response to rape and violence in K. Keay, ed., *Men, Women, and God* (Basingstoke, Hants, Marshall Pickering, 1987).
12. For example, J. Dobson, *Dare to Discipline* (Wheaton, IL, Tyndale House, 1973) and *Discipline While you can* (Eastbourne, Kingsway, 1978).
13. B. Campbell, *Unofficial Secrets* (London, Virago, 1988), p. 62.
14. See, for example, 'Women Abusers: the last taboo?', *Observer*, 8 April 1990.
15. De Mause's historical survey of the way children have been treated by their parents through history makes chilling reading. L. de Mause, ed., *The History of Childhood* (New York, Harper & Row, 1975).
16. See, for example, the *Independent*, 19 March 1990, and 'Heart of the Matter', BBC TV 22 July 1990.
17. See Campbell, *Unofficial Secrets*. My knowledge of events is gleaned from living in Cleveland at the time, and knowing some of the protagonists, as well as reading about it.
18. Hite, *The Hite Report on Male Sexuality*, pp. 329f. and 100f.
19. M. Hancock and K. Mains, *Child Sexual Abuse* (Crowborough, East Sussex, Highland Books, 1988; Wheaton, IL, Harold Shaw, 1987), p. 86.

11 WHOSE FAULT?

1. A serial sexual murderer in the United States, speaking before his execution; quoted in the *Observer*, 16 April 1989.
2. Pellauer et al., *Sexual Assault and Abuse*, p. 106.
3. In writing this, I did not anticipate the way senior Conservatives would try to deal with an increase in crime figures in September 1990. They suggested publicly that in many cases victims of theft were at fault, for leaving doors and windows unlocked. However, I still do not think that most people's first reaction is to blame the victim.
4. Brown and Parker in Brown and Bohn, *Christianity, Patriarchy, and Abuse*, p. 4. Their article is highly critical of theories of the atonement on these grounds, to the point where they find it hard to continue as Christians. Similar themes are explored in the context of a theological response to HIV/AIDS in J. Woodward, ed., *Embracing the Chaos* (London, SPCK, 1990).
5. D. Soelle, *Suffering* (London, Darton, Longman & Todd; Philadelphia, Fortress, 1975), p. 178.
6. H. Kushner, *When Bad Things Happen to Good People* (London, Pan; New York, Schocken Books, 1981), pp. 99-100.
7. ibid., pp. 143, 111.
8. M. Engel, in M. Engel and S. Thistlethwaite, eds., *Lift Every Voice* (New York, Harper & Row, 1990), pp. 318ff.
9. Fortune, *Sexual Violence*, pp. 63ff.
10. Pellauer et al., *Sexual Assault and Abuse*, p. 107.
11. Fortune, *Sexual Violence*, pp. 86, 119.
12. Pellauer et al., *Sexual Assault and Abuse*, p. 102.
13. The *Independent*, 4 February 1990. Other legal reasons were given for this, but the message the sentences gave was that rape was less important than burglary. Following this case, a change in the law allowed for appeal against sentences thought too low. The rape victim, Jill Saward, reveals just how great the trauma actually was in *Rape — My Story* (London, Bloomsbury, 1990).
14. R. Williams, 'Penance in the Penitentiary', lecture in Grendon Prison, 16 March 1989.

12 RESTORING THE IMAGE

1. Julian of Norwich, quoted in Nelson, *The Intimate Connection*, p. 24.
2. M. Eichler, *The Double Standard* (London, Croom Helm, 1980; New York, St Martin's Press, 1979), p. 92.
3. Fortune, *Sexual Violence*, pp. 30ff and 105ff.
4. ibid., p. 101.
5. Rousseau and Gallagher, *Sex is Holy*, p. 116.

Notes

6. V. Zundel, 'Carbon Dating'.
7. J. Spong, *Living in Sin?* (New York, Harper & Row, 1988), pp. 167, 173. For Dominian, see for example, *Marriage, Faith and Love* (London, Darton, Longman & Todd, 1981; New York, Crossroad, 1982) and *Proposals for a New Sexual Ethic* (London, Darton, Longman & Todd, 1977). See also S. Dowell, *They Two Shall Become One* (London, Collins, 1990) for a Christian feminist perspective on monogamy.
8. Brod, *A Mensch Among Men*, pp. 3-4.
9. Hite, *The Hite Report on Male Sexuality*, p. 60.
10. Wise and Stanley, *Georgie Porgie*, p. 200.
11. R. Coward, 'High Time Men Changed', *New Internationalist*, September 1987.
12. H. Oppenheimer, *The Hope of Happiness* (London and Philadelphia, SCM/TPI, 1983), p. 94.
13. Nelson, *The Intimate Connection*, p. 64.
14. Rousseau and Gallagher, *Sex is Holy*, pp. 8-9.
15. Nelson, *The Intimate Connection*, p. 26.
16. P. Moss and M. Fonda, *Work and the Family* (Aldershot, Hants, Temple Smith, 1980; Mystic, CT, Lawrence Verry, 1981), p. 8.
17. *Faith in the City*, p. 60.
18. A. Dworkin, *Our Blood* (London, Women's Press; New York, Harper & Row, 1976), p. 87.

Further Reading

The list given below offers a starting point for those who wish to explore more deeply the themes in *Distorted Images*. It is not comprehensive.

Books marked * have a Christian or religious perspective.

Women in society
Chodorow, N., *The Reproduction of Mothering*. Berkeley, CA, University of California Press, 1978.

Cline, S. and Spender, D., *Reflecting Men*. London, Deutsch, 1986; New York, Holt, Henry & Co., 1987.

Coward, R., *Female Desires*. London, Paladin; New York, Grove Press, 1985.

Dinnerstein, D., *The Rocking of the Cradle*. London, Souvenir Press, 1976.

*Dowell, S. and Hurcombe, L., *Dispossessed Daughters of Eve*. London, SPCK, 1987.

French, M., *Beyond Power*. London, Cape; New York, Ballantine Books, 1986.

*Furlong, M., ed., *Feminine in the Church*. London, SPCK, 1984.

*Furlong, M., ed., *Mirror to the Church*. London, SPCK, 1988.

Hite, S., *Women and Love*. London, Viking; New York, St Martin's Press, 1989.

*Joseph, A., ed., *Through the Devil's Gateway*. London, SPCK, 1990.

*Maitland, S., *A Map of the New Country*. London and Boston, Routledge & Kegan Paul, 1983.

Oakley, A., *Subject Women*. London, Collins; New York, Pantheon Books, 1981.

Rich, A., *Of Woman Born*. London, Virago; New York, Bantam Books, 1977.

Rogers, B., *Men Only*. London, Pandora, 1988.

Segal, L., *Is the Future Female?* London, Virago, 1987; New York, Peter Bedrick Books, 1988.

Smith, J., *Misogynies*. London, Faber & Faber, 1989.

Spender, D., *Man-Made Language*. London and Boston, Routledge & Kegan Paul, 1980.

Spender, D., *Invisible Women*. London and New York, Writers & Readers, 1982.

Wise, S. and Stanley, L., *Georgie Porgie*. London, Pandora, 1987.

Further Reading

Men in Society
Arcana, J., *Every Mother's Son*. London, Women's Press, 1983; Seattle, WA, Seal Press—Feminist, 1986.

*Brod, H., ed., *A Mensch among Men*. Freedom, CA, The Crossing Press, 1988.

Easthope, A., *What a Man's Gotta Do*. London, Collins, 1986; Winchester, MA, Unwin Hyman, 1990.

Ehrenreich, B., *The Hearts of Men*. London, Pluto Press, 1985; New York, Doubleday, 1984.

Ford, A., *Men*. London, Weidenfeld & Nicolson, 1985.

Ingham, M., *Men*. London, Century, 1984.

Jackson, B., *Fatherhood*. London, George Allen & Unwin, 1983.

Korda, M., *Male Chauvinism!* London, Hodder & Stoughton, 1975; New York, Ballantine Books, 1979.

Metcalf, A. and Humphries, M., *The Sexuality of Men*. London, Pluto Press, 1985.

*Nelson, J., *The Intimate Connection*. Philadelphia, Westminster, 1988.

Willis, P., *Learning to Labour*. London, Saxon House; Lexington, MA, Lexington Books, 1977.

*Wren, B., *What Language Shall I Borrow?* London, SCM; New York, Crossroad, 1989.

Sex and sexuality
*Avis, P., *Eros and the Sacred*. London, SPCK; Wilton, CT, Morehouse, 1989.

*Cotter, J., *Pleasure, Pain and Passion*. Leeds, Cairns Publications, 1988.

*Dowell, S., *They Two Shall Be One*. London, Collins, 1990.

Hite, S., *The Hite Report on Male Sexuality*. London, Macdonald; New York, Alfred A. Knopf, 1981.

Hite, S., *The Hite Report*. London, Pandora 1989; New York, Dell, 1987.

Lee, C., *The Ostrich Position*. London, Unwin; New York, Writers & Readers, 1986.

Lee, C., *Friday's Child*. Wellingborough, Thorsons, 1988.

*Nelson, J., *Embodiment*. Minneapolis, MN, Augsburg, 1979.

Parrinder, G., *Sex in the World's Religions*. London, Sheldon; New York, Oxford University Press, 1980.

*Rousseau, M. and Gallagher, C., *Sex Is Holy*. New York, Amity House, 1986.

*Spong, J., *Living in Sin?* New York, Harper & Row, 1988.

Vance, C., ed., *Pleasure and Danger: Exploring Female Sexuality*. London, Routledge & Kegan Paul, 1984; New York, Routledge, Chapman & Hall, 1990.

Pornography, Sexual Violence and Abuse
Brownmiller, S., *Against our Will*. London, Penguin, 1980; New York, Bantam Books, 1976.

151

*Bussert, J., *Battered Women*. Lutheran Church in America, 1986.

Cameron, D. and Frazer, E., *The Lust to Kill*. Cambridge, Polity Press; New York University Press, 1987.

Campbell, B., *Unofficial Secrets*. London, Virago, 1988.

Chester, G. and Dickey, J., eds., *Feminism and Censorship*. Bridport, Dorset, Prism Press, 1988.

*Court, J., *Pornography: A Christian Critique*. Exeter, Paternoster, 1980.

Driver, E. and Doisen, A., *Child Sexual Abuse*. London, Macmillan; New York University Press, 1989.

Dworkin, A., *Pornography*. London, The Women's Press, 1981; New York, E. P. Dutton, 1989.

*Fortune, M., *Sexual Violence*. New York, The Pilgrim Press, 1983.

Griffin, S., *Pornography and Silence*. London, Women's Press; New York, Harper & Row, 1981.

*Horton, A. and Williamson, J., eds., *Abuse and Religion*. Lexington, MA, Lexington Books, 1988.

Jeffreys, S., *Anticlimax*. London, Women's Press, 1990.

Kappeler, S., *Pornography and Representation*. Cambridge, Polity Press; Minneapolis, University of Minnesota Press, 1986.

Kelly, L., *Surviving Sexual Violence*. Cambridge, Polity Press, 1988.

*Pellauer, M., Chester, B. and Boyajian, J., *Sexual Assault and Abuse*. New York, Harper & Row, 1987.

*Saward, J., *Rape — My Story*. London, Bloomsbury, 1990.

Organizations which may be of help include:

The Institute for the Study of Christianity and Sexuality, Oxford House, Derbyshire Street, London E2 6HG, Tel. 071 739 1249. ISCS aims to deepen the understanding of the links between the Christian faith and sexuality.

CWIRES (Christian Women's Information and Resources), c/o Blackfriars, St Giles, Oxford, OX1 3LY, has a wide ranging collection of books and articles on women and the churches and feminist theology. It produces a reading list on Women and Christianity, and an information sheet on relevant groups.